A CHRISTIAN GUIDE TO

DIVORCE & REMARRIAGE

JOHN DEVRIES

A CHRISTIAN GUIDE TO

DIVORCE &
REMARRIAGE

A SCRIPTURAL EXPOSITION

TATE PUBLISHING & *Enterprises*

Published by Tate Publishing & Enterprises, LLC
127 E. Trade Center Terrace | Mustang, Oklahoma 73064 USA
1.888.361.9473 | www.tatepublishing.com

Tate Publishing is committed to excellence in the publishing industry. The company reflects the philosophy established by the founders, based on Psalm 68:11,
"The Lord gave the word and great was the company of those who published it."

Book design copyright © 2011 by Tate Publishing, LLC. All rights reserved.
Cover design by Amber Gulliat
Interior design by Sarah Kirchen

Published in the United States of America

ISBN: 978-1-61346-430-4
1. Religion / Christian Life / Love & Marriage
2. Religion / Christian Church / Leadership
11.08.19

ACKNOWLEDGMENTS

To the LORD of Glory, Majesty, and Honor, who is righteous, gracious, and merciful in all of His dealings with man. I praise you, oh God and Father of our LORD Jesus Christ. You set captives free and open prison doors. You are the liberator from bondage. You anoint Your children with the oil of gladness, dressing them with the garment of praise, destroying the spirit of heaviness. Your truths understood and applied to life's difficulties allow us to taste just a glimpse of what heaven will be like. You are the righteous judge of all the earth.

And:

To my encouraging, patient wife, Siony, who has sacrificially set me free as "unto the LORD" on many occasions to write.

To all of the true believers in our Savior Jesus Christ, who struggle with marriage issues and desire to know what God expects and directs us to do in difficult circumstances.

Thank you to our "Timothys": Pst. Jamie and Sherrie Jenicek. To "Wellsprings," for having stood the test of time to be faithful in your love for Siony and I. Thank you, Julie Hjelvik, for always encouraging us on. A special thanks to Arne and Kathie Bryan of Prayer Canada, our teacher friends Dr. Kevin and Barb. Thanks to our fellow board member, Don Fultz, who has prophesied that I would write books some day.

You and many others have always encouraged me. A special thanks to our Philippine covenant apostle ministry friends, Ernesto and Sally Balili. We thank the LORD for the many churches and ministries He has allowed you to touch and oversee. May our gracious Holy God bless and reward all of you. We love you.

TABLE OF CONTENTS

FOREWORD

I have known Bishop and Apostle John DeVries and his apostolic anointed ministry since the early eighties. For more than twenty-five years, we've been partners as covenant brothers with mutual responsibilities, with accountability to each other and to our God-given five-fold ministry churches.

In this connection, I am endorsing his powerful and eye-opening books, *Christian Divorce and Remarriage* and *Fivefold Ministry Churches as well* to you, the reader. I have read, re-read, and thoroughly checked and studied all the scriptures and truths presented in these books. As his co-apostle and partner in our ministries, his books have blessed me greatly. *Christian Divorce and Remarriage* exposes the many Bible truths mostly missed by so many believers and churches.

I believe that if one reads this presentation while personally reviewing the scriptures referenced, they will be rewarded with a great gain of understanding. Bereans were more noble than those in Thessalonica, because they personally verified whether the things Paul ta--ght were scripturally correct. (Act 17:11) These books will help you in your ministry as a leader in God's kingdom. I challenge all readers to pass these books along to your loved friends and ministry partners.

—Bishop Ernesto Balili, Apostle/President, King Jesus Christian Fellowship [KJCFI] Churches and Ministers and associated churches and ministries in the Philippines.

Chairman of Apostolic Five-Fold Churches, Inc. [AFFCI]

Chairman, Metro Cagayan de Oro City Ministers Fellowship, Inc [MCMFI]

INTRODUCTION

Marital problems are common. All of us require answers to be correct before the LORD in how we handle these problems in a godly fashion. This is especially true when the problems end in a divorce. Divorce is always attended with pain and devastation. This tearing always includes far reaching relational and practical problems. The total picture is similar to the decease of a loved one, but the funeral never ends. The corpse is still walking around, affecting one's life.

A larger consequence beyond these realities is an overshadowing factor which always attends the true believer. How does one stand with the LORD Jesus Christ and heaven's throne? We will struggle when we are on an insecure terrain, due to not knowing how our resulting broken marriage affects our relationship with Him. Our faith walk will be disturbed when we cannot "lift up our eyes unto the hills from whence comes our strength," due to guilt and failure.

One must know what their godly rights are in the LORD's sight, to continue with a faith walk. Having experienced this dilemma as a church pastor has caused me to deeply dig into the Scriptures to find God's answers to these questions. He has the answers when others do not. One must have a sure knowledge of God's Word to know their course and rights. God's Word is complete and provides these answers. Unfortunately the common scriptural answers most hold are incomplete and inconsistent with what the apostle Paul said to his ministry student, Timothy: "All scripture is given by inspiration of God, and is profitable for doctrine, for reproof, for correction, for instruction in righteousness (2 Tim. 3:16). Many scriptures and doctrinal truths are commonly overlooked.

When we are faced with humanly impossible situations involving marital relationships, the true child of God will struggle with the question of what is spiritually and biblically correct in their response to these circumstances. A thought that will heavily weigh on them, will be how their heavenly Father and Savior will view the decisions made and actions taken.

This always enters into the equation. Many questions enter into the equation of difficult marriage circumstances. Will a righteous God condemn me for divorcing from a partner who is unaccountable for wrongful actions or inactions? Does the marriage vow taken bind me to an intolerable union, where my partner refuses to address areas of wrong doing?

Am I tied to a ball and chain relationship regardless of my husband or wife's actions or inactions? A marriage torn with strife due to someone not wanting to discuss and resolve difficulties in a godly manner, disallows a life of peace. This certainly does not bring about the Bible picture of God's Kingdom in the home, a Kingdom of righteousness, peace and joy in the Holy Ghost. The Holy Ghost is the author of peace which all believers have a right to, and will exist when all parties involved will prayerfully discuss rights and wrongs.

Due to understanding the heartaches and devastation involved in the divorce of a genuine Christian, this book is written. Having found the answers from God's Word as to what one should do in the case of Christian marital problems, a possible divorce or potential remarriage, I herein share these scriptural and textual findings.

When reading this presentation, have your Bible open and read any scriptures referred to in context. May our faith and beliefs be anchored to God's Word and void the opinions of man.

—John DeVries

POEM

Oh love that's gained and love that's gone,

What joys destroyed, and what went wrong?

A wedding dream now shattered, torn

The tux and gown that once adorned

The wedding day with dreams of hopes and bliss

Crushed to the earth, what went amiss?

Yet from divorce's grave I ask, is there yet hope,

Am I yet equal to the task, beyond
this darkness where I grope,

For love and life, as husband to a new wed wife?

To love again from failure's banks, without a mask

A marriage that that is void of tears and strife?

And from a torn and pain-filled heart I ask,

Dear God what is my right before your sight?

Show me thy way, when none can help but thee.

And by thy grace show me thy truth,

Come be my help, now comfort and deliver me.

Oh Jesus grant your mercy LORD,

For you alone can heal my heart.

Grant to me a new born day, a dawn with hope,

A fading darkness lightened, life with a brand new start.

Show me thy way, restore my broken heart

Up from the ashes I now stand, your truth has set me free.

Thy Word did heal, speak, comfort and delivered me.

New sight is mine, praise God, I now can see.

I praise my Savior LORD whom by His grace,

Revealed His truth, has granted me fresh eyes,

By understanding from His Word I'm freed

From sorrows blinding shadowed banks I rise.

—JDV

MARITAL PAIN
AND DIVORCE

Heartaches by the Dozen,
Troubles by the Score

You are a Christian, believing in God. You believe the Bible and sermons preached on Sundays. You made your marriage vows before the LORD to a spouse you loved and believed in. But now you are battling some horrible factors in your marriage, seemingly destroying your person and existence. Pain, abuse, and heartache are the constant companions of your mind. Unreasonable and uncontrolled anger are choking the lifeblood out of you. Your personal inability to live with the anger directed towards you has become intolerable.

Love seems to have shredded. There is a wall of painful silence and a torn peace where love and joy once blissfully blossomed between you and your spouse. The joy has long since evacuated, only to be replaced with an imprisoning ball and chain existence. You and your spouse are unable to discuss problems with each other in a reasonable fashion. You have a partner who is unwilling to discuss these problems for whatever reason.

Has your marriage degenerated to a "bad roommate" relationship? Is there no positive resolution in sight? The greater questions are: does the Bible have answers for these circumstances? Does God care? What does one do in these circumstances, and yet be right with God? Does God speak and give directions to resolving such a tangled mess?

Yes! He does!

Yes, our loving, holy God does speak to and has answers as to how we should handle difficult relationship matters. The contents of this book are for the genuine God-seeking Christian, the genuine believing child of God who is looking for answers. This is for those who need Bible-based, textually correct and clearly set out, theologically sound answers, according to God's Word. This is for those who are not content with mere opinions, but need clearly set out scriptural answers. This is for the Godly souls who will apply themselves to researching the truth of this topic biblically.

This is for those who deeply need to know how God really views these matters, and when they find the answers will act according to their findings.

This limited number of people will eventually live at peace with a clear conscience. Potential joy on the horizon will be theirs, regardless of what the road of tomorrow brings. They will have peace. In time they will experience a liberty and healing within, whether in the restoration of the marriage, separation, divorce, or remarriage.

When almost half of church attendees are touched by the pain and trauma of divorce and its related issues, one would think that any scriptures regarding this topic would be exhausted and fully studied. When we consider the pain and world of heartache involved in marriage problems, affecting the saints who are God's greatest treasure on earth, one would think all ministers would have studied this topic in depth and preached all textually needed truth.

A fully understood, scripturally balanced knowledge, associated with proper actions, will avoid huge numbers of divorces. Many marriages headed for the rocks could become havens of health and joy when proper knowledge is applied. The prophet, Hosea, clearly states the reality of God's heart touching this and other topics. In Hosea 6:4 the prophet mourns: "My people are destroyed for lack of knowledge." True Bible knowledge and knowing how our living God tells us to deal with this topic will bring a great inner peace. Clear knowledge will break the chains of false condemnation and wrongful guilt. When one knows God's truths for conduct, appropriate actions will result in a clear conscience when dealing with any matter. A liberty of joy and freedom will overtake us. Genuine healing, due to a sure knowledge of our godly rights and decisions before the LORD, will result in peace with joy. What the prophet David said shall be our portion: "His truth shall be thy shield and buckler" (Psalm. 91:4). Truth is always a garment of defense from erroneous condemnation.

Only by a sure knowledge of God's Word can we have a clear conscience when dealing with our spouse. If we deny our knowledge and conscience, we will forever walk through life pulling a heavy chain of guilt.

Guilt

Guilt comes from our "conscience." Our conscience will either approve or accuse us. The apostle Paul wrote, "Which show the work of the law written in their hearts, their conscience also bearing witness, and their thoughts the mean while accusing or else excusing one another" (Romans 2:15). The genuine Christian, after having experienced being born again spiritually, has God's Holy Spirit joined to their spirit being. Our human spirit is our "conscience." The apostle Paul explained, "I say the truth in Christ, I lie not, my conscience also bearing me witness in the Holy Ghost" (Romans 9:1). We can only experience a clear and non-condemning "conscience" when we know our dealings are based on truthful actions. We find this interesting biblical statement about our conscience, written by Solomon: "The spirit of man is the candle of the LORD, searching all the inward parts of the belly" (being) (Proverbs 20:27).

In the tripartite of man, the body is easy to understand. Our soul is made up of the combined mind, will, and emotions. Our "spirit man," commonly referred to as our "conscience," is the mental referee approving or disapproving moral matters. When the Holy Spirit of God joins with our human spirit at the time of being "born of the

Spirit," our spirit is illuminated to a greater level of discernment as to moral issues and truth. This is due to God's Holy Spirit joining Himself to our human spirit (Romans 8:11–16).

Knowing truth is of mega-importance to any matter we are involved with. We must understand what our LORD and Savior Jesus Christ said, "Ye shall know the truth, and the truth shall make you free" (John 8:32). What is the truth, especially as to this topic under focus, which is so relevant and important?

Having walked through the valley of the death of a marriage, I personally was forced to search the scriptures as never before, finding light and life, and answers to the questions storming in my mind. Our God is a righteous judge of all the earth. Here in this life, and in eternity future, when we will all be standing before His throne, He deals with holy integrity in the affairs of man. He is the defender of the wounded. I needed genuine answers as we all do when trapped in this difficult and tearing valley of struggles.

One of the great difficulties we encounter when caught in the vice of a marriage breakdown is the absence of righteous and holy counseling availability. What if you are a minister and your spouse refuses to attend a marriage counseling session with those who know you best, crying "foul" due to the suspicion of bias? What if the ministries you know suggest you see some professional counselors with professional fees attached, and do not get "in the trenches" with you at this time of great need? If this is the case, I suggest you look for a different church or pastor.

What if the highly recommended person where you attend has a one line answer, being "just forgive and all will become well," refusing to address issues which exist? Counselors giving counsel without absolutes of right or wrong bear consequences to both parties. I have personally experienced this and have counseled many who are victims of this wrongful type of questionable counseling.

Worse yet, what if the counselor or pastor has a limited and wrong scriptural bias, where their entire pivotal mind set is unjust, due to a lack of Bible knowledge? Now you are being guided by a "bent light" into realms of darkness. Now you are the blind being led by the blind, and both are heading for the ditch (Luke 6:39). We must personally become knowledgeable of God's Word in this matter.

What if the counselor has a bias that there is no acceptable reason for divorce? With such a person, there is a choke chain on any future hope. With such an opinion in counseling, no matter how much one is willing to address wrong, there is no real defense from a spouse bent on unacceptable behavior.

Recently I purchased a book where three known evangelical Bible scholars presented their slightly differing views about remarriage after divorce in today's church. All had some obvious good insights, but all missed major scriptural truths while dealing with this topic. Generally speaking they hold a one text theology versus the several truths and Bible texts relating to this topic.

Most held the viewpoint that only via the death of a spouse was re-marriage an acceptable potential. They presented that divorce was a possibility if proven adultery was involved; however, remarriage was highly questionable, even with a proven adulterous spouse being divorced.

They neglected covering the other truths which greatly affect this topic from a large scriptural base available from both the Old and New testaments. Topics such as:

- Covenant and covenant breaking.

- Church eldership involvement.

- Church judgment of resisting implacable claimed believers.

- Distinguishing the differing Bible dealings for two believers and a believer with an unbeliever.

- Believers married to difficult unbelievers.

- The differing rules which apply as to remarriage when there are two or one believers involved.

- Claimed believers disregarding Bible principles of conduct and church accountability.

- Church and elders' responsibilities in intervention when problems exist.

- The believer's responsibilities when problems arise, before God and man.

We need answers as to what one must do when facing marriage problems, knowing there is justice and freedom from a wrongful relationship, while being right with God as well. We must know there is a holy, God-provided justice. We must find God's directions and apply these by the clear, holy light from God's Word.

In Troubled Waters, Yet at Peace

Is it possible for a Christian to be at peace with God while passing through the fires of separation, divorce, and remarriage? Yes, it is. In fact, our God has called us to be at peace. Jesus said, "Peace I leave with you; my peace I give to you. Not as the world gives do I give to you. Let not your hearts be troubled, neither let them be afraid" (John 14:27). This "let not" is our responsibility. Often we are caught in unrest due to not doing our part and responsibility. "Let not" is our responsibility.

The problem encountered with most believers is that they "cannot" be at peace. Usually this is due to being insecure as to what is right and acceptable before our God. In dealing with this most difficult issue involving separation, divorce, or remarriage, one must know their scriptural position and what the Lord tells us in this matter. When one is on a sure ground of knowledge as to their godly and scriptural responsibilities and rights, sure steps will follow bringing peace within.

This does not mean that we will not be faced with pain, sorrow, or heartache in the soul and emotional realm. Only the Lord can minister to that. However, having an understanding of what our rights are and what a proper response to our circumstances is, will promote healing. This is where godly counsel with genuine knowledge will be of great help. Mighty eternal God, by Your grace, raise up these knowledgeable ministry counselors!

Few churches readily set out their beliefs about this subject. Fewer still present a balanced, multiple scripturally balanced understanding of the many factors which affect this subject.

Divorced Christians and Pain

I see many people living a wrongful slow death of pain, struggling in their marriages. Often this is due to them being bound in their circumstances by a falsehood due to the consequence of a lack of knowledge. A hopeless guilt prevails due to them lacking knowing of their rights before God. The studied truths set forth herein will alleviate this needless struggle.

There Is Hope for the Separated or Divorced Christian

There is a holy course of action for those living in pain. God's Holy Word provides this hope. Unresolved marriage problems are a tremendously painful fact that attend many believers' lives. When divorce results, the sorrows and pain attached damages the husband and wife for a lifetime. As well, this affects untold numbers of children, family, and friends, leaving many scarred lives. Often this pain does not subside in those affected, until "death do us part" from pain and sorrow.

The side effects of divorce can leave a trail with many interconnecting paths of separation, within families, the church believers they fellowshipped with, and particularly the siblings.

Divorce: Avoided and Ignored Scriptures

When we ignore Bible scriptures, the end result is devastating. The biblical, historical account of the rich man and Lazarus that the LORD Jesus spoke of ended with the rich man lifting up his eyes in "hell," the "end all" of a terrible place to open one's eyes (Luke 16:20–25). Many believers also ignore important scriptures, the result being that some will open their eyes some morning facing a hell on earth in their marriage.

Ignoring scriptures is much like the little lady who had a nearly new car coming to a grinding, smoking halt as she was driving down the road. She was enjoying a beautiful ride on a sunny morning in her recently purchased automobile when suddenly, the ride stopped and a tow truck was called to attend and get it to a garage. The mechanic asked if she knew what the little red light indicator, warning "Oil needed" on the dash, was for. She said, "I was wondering about that." Many wonder about that but do not research to find out, until their marriage comes to a screeching halt.

There are two scriptural reasons divorce is permissible, although the second reason is somewhat interconnected to the first. The first reason is clear and undeniable without room for debate. However, I ask why are the following scriptures are rarely heard as a sermon topic, while they affect so many people?

For example, "And I say unto you, whosoever shall put away his wife, except it be for fornication, and shall marry commits adultery: and whoso marries her who is put away doth commit adultery." Is this a Christ-stated exception which allows for a scriptural divorce. (Matthew 19:9)?

"And Jesus answered and said, Verily I say unto you, There is no man that hath left house, or brethren, or sisters, or father, or mother, or wife, or children, or lands, for my sake, and the gospel's" (Mark 10:29).

Leave a wife and that's for Christ's sake? How does that work?

"But to the rest speak I, not the LORD: If any brother hath a wife that believeth not, and she be pleased to dwell with him, let him not put her away. And the woman who hath a husband that believeth not, and if he be pleased to dwell with her, let her not leave him." (1 Corinthians 7:12–13) What if it is clear that the unbeliever is not pleased? Is this a legitimate God-sanctioned reason for leaving a marriage?

God has directions for dealing with all issues of life. These include marriage difficulties. Our LORD Jesus spoke to this matter several times. Unfortunately most preachers and believers have disregarded His statements. The result is a world of hurt for many, which always accompanies the fruit of disregarding God's Word.

GOD'S INSTRUCTIONS IN MARRIAGE DIFFICULTIES

Christ-Given Instructions

Jesus, the LORD of the Church, clearly taught:

> Moreover if thy brother shall trespass against thee, go and tell him his fault between thee and him alone: if he shall hear thee, thou hast gained thy brother. But if he will not hear thee, then take with thee one or two more, that in the mouth of two or three witnesses every word may be established. And if he shall neglect to hear them, tell it unto the church: but if he neglect to hear the church, let him be unto thee as a heathen man and a publican.
>
> Matthew 18:15–17

Has this scriptural directive been brought to you, who are struggling with marital issues? I have rarely seen this acted on or heard this taught. Do these scriptures apply now today? Is this to be applied in our New Testament churches? The intent is to gain a lost brother.

Then the Words from the apostle Paul, which are divinely inspired, also speak to relational matters and specifically, marriage relationships. The apostle Paul taught, "But if the unbelieving depart, let him depart. A brother or a sister is not under bondage in such cases: but God hath called us to peace" (1 Corinthians 7:15). Does God make provision under some circumstances for one to be freed from a marriage with peace of mind? How does that work? "Not in bondage"—does this mean one is totally freed from the marriage? Is one freed with the right to marry again? Yes!

"Art thou bound unto a wife? Seek not to be loosed. Art thou loosed from a wife? Seek not a wife. But and if thou marry, thou hast not sinned; and if a virgin marry, she hath not sinned" (1 Corinthians 7:27–28). Loosed from a wife; but if one marries again, have they not sinned? How and when do these scriptures apply?

Does God Himself Divorce People?

God spoke of Him divorcing people long before the New Testament times. God's Word includes, "And I said after she had done all these things, Turn thou unto me. But she returned not. And her treacherous sister Judah saw it. And I saw, when for all the causes whereby backsliding Israel committed adultery I had put her away, and given her a bill of divorce" (Jeremiah 3:7–8). Is this our God, the God of Abraham, Isaac and Jacob? Is this our covenant-making God divorcing Israelites, His covenant people?

By their partaking in the vow of circumcision, they had said yes LORD, you are our God and we will walk before you. This act of obedience demanded by the LORD, was man's statement of yes, I accept your covenant. Those who rejected this act of circumcision were also denied God's covenant relationship and were cut off from His people (Genesis 17:14) Similarly we state our vows in the marriage covenant with our ring exchange. By our subsequent actions, we can also break our marriage covenant. Many in Israel, circumcised and all were cut off from our God since their actions caused a rejection of their person. They were judged by God Almighty as covenant breakers. (Jeremiah 11:10)

Again in Isaiah God tells us, "Thus says the LORD, Where is the bill of your mother's divorcement, whom I have put away? Or which of my creditors is it to which I have sold you? Behold, for your iniquities have ye sold yourselves, and for your transgressions is your mother put away." (Isaiah 50:1) Did God really mean and do this? Did He really divorce these Israelites? Was this some poetic language or did our God actually divorce these people?

The result of this what Isaiah said, is memorialized in the following scriptures.

Except the LORD of hosts had left unto us a very small remnant, we should have been as Sodom, and we should have been like unto Gomorrah. Hear the word of the LORD, ye rulers of Sodom; give ear unto the law of our God, ye people of Gomorrah. To what purpose is the multitude of your sacrifices unto me? Says the LORD: I am full of the burnt offerings of rams, and the fat of fed beasts; and I delight not in the blood of bullocks, or of lambs, or of the goats.

Isaiah 1:9–11

Our God clearly states that a limited remnant number of His covenant people remained that He did not destroy in judgment. These people Isaiah referred to discarded their salvation status and eternal God relationship. These people are referred to by the apostle Paul in 1 Corinthians 10:5. Our God expressed His disdain of these past covenant people, demonstrated by their bodies being strewn throughout the dessert without burial dignities. He rejected their religiosity. In contrast, consider how the LORD cared for the Moses funeral and burial, when He personally buried Moses with respect of his person (Deuteronomy 34:4–6).

Traditions of Men

May we avoid being guilty of what our LORD Jesus reprimanded the Pharisees for during His days on earth. Our LORD Jesus told them, "Ye made the commandment of God of none effect by your tradition. Ye hypocrites, well did Esaias prophesy of you, saying, This people draws nigh unto me with their mouth, and honors me with their lips; but their heart is far from me." (Matthew 15:6-8).

My apostle friend, Ernesto Balili, from Mindanao in the Philippine Islands, said this well: "This means that any tradition, no matter how good it seems to be, made by men or a church that alters the truths of the Bible, is an enemy of God and His holy Word." Traditions will pass, but God's Word will stand forever. His Word is always fighting opinions and traditions opposed to Him."

May we consider all relevant scriptures touching the topic of divorce and remarriage! If we do not, our views and catechisms are wrong, since God's Word is complete and will stand forever. When these scriptures are avoided and ignored, our incomplete counsel and views are like trying to complete a puzzle with incomplete pieces.

Revelation

When studying Bible truth about divorce and marriage, as in all matters of life and relationships, whether toward God or man, we need holy revelation.

The apostle Paul prayed that the spirit of wisdom and revelation might come upon the church of Ephesus, "That the God of our LORD Jesus Christ, the Father of glory, may give unto you the spirit of wisdom and revelation in the knowledge of him" (Ephesians 1:17).

True revelation knowledge is simply God's Word truths revealed to the church. All truths are written and can be found in God's Word, the Bible. Holy revelation brings understanding within the hearts of men.

Many vastly important truths written in God's Word are simply read over and are not seen, as to their meaning and value. These truths are revealed to the searching one when they gain insight by the spirit of revelation as they ponder and weigh what is read. Then the obscure becomes simple and the revealed obvious, bringing life.

This also applies when dealing with Christian divorce and remarriage, as this topic is outlined herein. The truths focused on have always been there, but were simply "read over." These truths set one free, and will break mental chains and false guilt (John 8:32). In this "latter days" church, many great truths that were once lost are unfolding, becoming clear and visible. These truths were read over and overlooked for centuries. To demonstrate this, consider the following examples.

Other Revealed Truths

Many Christians today understand the importance of being "born again" and know this as an experiential event. This is subsequent to facing sin within and repenting of personal sin. Paul taught the sequence of how this takes place in Ephesians 1:13, "In whom ye also trusted, after that ye heard the word of truth, the gospel of your salvation: in whom also after that ye believed, ye were sealed with that Holy Spirit of promise."

Paul clearly taught that one must hear the truth to believe and after believing, one is sealed with the Holy Spirit. This does not happen because someone sprinkles a baby or baptizes an unrepentant, unbelieving person. In Romans 10:14–15, Paul states, "How then shall they call on him in whom they have not believed? And how shall they believe in him of whom they have not heard? And how shall they hear without a preacher? And how shall they preach, except they be sent? As it is written, how beautiful are the feet of them that preach the gospel of peace, and bring glad tidings of good things!"

Many churches do not teach this Bible truth, telling people to put their faith in their infant baptism and that they belong to "the" genuinely right church. The result is an insecure faith, with no sure knowledge or joy of salvation.

One must personally repent of sin, placing their faith in Jesus, His life, death and the cross, and His shed blood, for their sins. Then we must accept the Lordship of Christ over our lives, following our placing faith in His atonement at the cross as payment for our personal sins. Many have left denominational background churches because those churches do not teach this clearly set out Bible truth. Our LORD said that if a person is not born again, they cannot enter the kingdom of God (John 3:3, 5).

Of course, we know that some may say they believe and teach this, while many church catechisms teach this topic in a completely wrong manner, lacking revelation. Many attach this to infant baptism or to some rite of membership. Many attach this to what others do for us, while the truth is that this can only be accomplished directly between God and us personally.

Huge numbers of true believers, having personally experienced being "born again," know the genuine presence of the Holy Spirit, having genuine peace within their hearts. They now look forward to heaven and God's throne instead of living in the fear of not knowing if they will even be accepted.

The true believer says Amen and Hallelujah to John 5:24, "Verily, verily, I say unto you, He that hears my Word, and believes on him that sent me, has everlasting life, and shall not come into condemnation; but is passed from death unto life." Should you not relate to this Bible text, you probably need to be born again.

Also, many believers today have received an experiential "baptism in the Holy Spirit," subsequent to their new birth experience. This experience brings one into a much deeper involvement with the Holy Spirit, although this is denied by many old denominational churches. (Acts 19:2, 8:17, 11:16, 2:4, 8).

Wrong Church Rules

Wrong doctrine and Bible theology have caused huge problems through the centuries. Correcting our opinions to align with true scriptural writings is so imperative. This is the arena of life where the devil has caused huge deception causing death. There are many examples of this, such as many Catholics now understand that the apostle Peter was married. "Have we not power to lead about a sister, a wife, as well as other apostles, and as the brethren of the Lord, and Cephas (Peter)?" Also Matthew 1:30, "But Simon's (Peter) wife's mother lay sick of a fever, and at once they told Him about her" (1 Corinthians 9:5).

Wrong beliefs about this fact of Bible truth has caused numerous death and problems. The Word of God states all have the right to marriage, including apostles and all ministries. The choice to marry should never be a man-made or enforced limitation imposed on them who desire to serve in ministry. God's holy Word states that it is better to marry than have unfulfilled sexual desires met (1 Co. 7:9, 28). To initiate this rule as a celibacy demand upon those who wish to serve in ministry places an unnatural and unscriptural demand upon the priests and nuns. This is a major contributing cause for pedophilic and homosexual behavior experienced among the priesthood.

"Man's doctrine" is the root to the problems which the press and courts are dealing with, bringing shame to the gospel in open public view to the world.

This unscriptural celibacy law imposed on those wanting to be involved in priestly ministry is completely in opposition to God's Word: "But if you cannot restrain your desires, go ahead and marry—it is better to marry than to burn with passion" (1 Co. 7:9). This Bible statement is also Holy Spirit-inspired from the God Who created sex. Unnatural laws encourage wrong behavior. Lacking Bible knowledge produces a host of spiritual blindness with real life problems as a result, such as pedophilia, homosexual priests, and pregnant nuns behind cloistered doors with destroyed babies.

Many Catholics now understand that Jesus in the flesh had brothers and sisters. They understand the virgin birth was by the God-honored virgin Mary who, blessed and all, is a sinner saved by grace. She is not the "queen of heaven," although she is highly honored among women. "There came then his brethren and his mother, and, standing without, sent unto him, calling him. And the multitude sat about him, and they said unto him, Behold, thy mother and thy brethren without seek for thee" (Matthew 13:55–56; Mark 3:32–33).

I have the greatest respect for Mary who our LORD chose to birth the Savior. I so admire her godly person when I read how she responded to the state of her holy pregnancy. However, Mary was among those waiting in the upper room to receive the baptism of the Holy Spirit, as other believing Christians (Acts 1:13–14). Regardless of the honor bestowed upon her to birth the man child Jesus, as the angel told her "blessed art thou among women," she also belonged to the company of "all" who need redemption by Christ's blood (Luke 1:28). Romans 3:23 states, "For all have sinned, and come short of the glory of God." The only initially sinless person besides Adam and Eve was Jesus the Christ.

Reducing Divorce Statistics

To reduce divorce statistics, all churches and believers should have a balanced scriptural understanding of this topic. Biblical understanding of this immensely important topic will enable us to minister to those involved and eliminate much pain. As well, with a correct knowledge we would lower the divorce statistics among true believers. How important is that and how important are these believers?

The apostle, Peter, tells us of the value our God places on believers, "But ye are a chosen generation, a royal priesthood, an holy nation, a peculiar people; that ye should show forth the praises of him who hath called you out of darkness into his marvelous light" (1Peter 2:9).

The apostle, James, said, "Be patient therefore, brethren, unto the coming of the LORD. Behold, the husbandman waits for the precious fruit of the earth, and hath long patience for it" (James 5:7). They are extremely important to our LORD and must be to us as well. If not, be honest and get out of the ministry!

Minister and Ministry of God

May we have a heart of compassion for the weary and wounded among us. May we portray the Father's heart for His children. May we not just limit our efforts to the preaching of moral platitudes without demonstrating a genuine burden for the souls of the people. We must live out a depiction of a Christ pleasing holy life with love for the flock. This expressed love includes caring for their personal in home needs facing life's struggle areas. So many start out right but lose their focus. They degenerate to prioritizing the building up of church attendance and becoming money managers to sustain a profession and organization.

May we weep with those who weep and bear the burdens of the burdened. This is the portrayal of the Father's heart. Our LORD asked Peter, "Do you love me?" The direction given upon Peter's affirmative response was "feed my lambs and sheep" (John 21:15).

We as shepherds are to portray the heart and caring of the Creator shepherd. David observed a wondrous truth: "The LORD is my shepherd" (Psalm 23:1). Likewise, true shepherds of the church and ministry leadership should lead their sheep into green pastures beside still waters. Our LORD Jesus said that He is the good shepherd and lays His life down for the sheep. We in our ministry should do likewise. This shepherding must include dealing with painful marriage relationships and bringing righteous godliness into the believer's lives and families.

Today, the church and world need to see the shepherd who gently folds the lambs into his bosom, and knows his sheep by name. Isaiah 40:11 says, "He shall feed his flock like a shepherd: he shall gather the lambs with his arm, and carry them in his bosom, and shall gently lead those that are with young."

Shepherding includes bringing healing and binding up the wounds of the brokenhearted under the anointing, by the spirit of the LORD (Isaiah 61:1–2).

The Value of a True Believer

The church of the living God is the most precious entity in the universe. The true "born of the Spirit" believing person is destined to be the bride of Christ for eternity (Revelation 22:7). Heaven and earth shall pass away. These precious souls shall live forever to be with their LORD and Savior (Matthew 24:35, 2 Peter 3:13, James 5:7).

Whatever we do and say that affects these precious souls, either in a positive or negative manner, is hugely important in the eyes of the LORD. In the case of offensive words and actions, should these cause a child of God to stumble, our LORD Jesus said, "It were better for him that a millstone were hanged about his neck, and he be cast into the sea, than that he should offend one of these little ones" (Luke 17:2).

The Church

In this writing, it may appear that the author has a "baseball bat" bad attitude. It may seem like this writing is taking a baseball bat of destruction to the churches. This is not the case. Believers and the church need to understand and teach a balanced truth regarding God's directions as to dealing with marital problems. May we see a right heart and understanding demonstrated within the entire church. I agree with the apostle Paul and his view of the believing church, just as he expressed himself while writing to Corinth.

> Unto the church of God which is at Corinth, to them that are sanctified in Christ Jesus, called to be saints, with all that in every place call upon the name of Jesus Christ our LORD, both theirs and ours: Grace be unto you, and peace, from God our Father, and from the LORD Jesus Christ. I thank my God always on your behalf, for the grace of God which is given you by Jesus Christ; That in everything ye are enriched by him, in all utterance, and in all knowledge; Even as the testimony of Christ was confirmed in you: So that ye come behind in no gift; waiting for the coming of our LORD Jesus Christ: Who shall also confirm you unto the end, that ye may be blameless in the day of our LORD Jesus Christ."
>
> 1 Corinthians 2:1–8

All true believers, regardless of which church affiliation or denomination they belong to, are the "beloved saints." They are the coming "bride company" of our LORD and Savior, Jesus Christ. They are the "fruit of the earth, and beloved" (James 5:7).

We must be armed with balanced Bible truth. My dear and holy beloved fellow ministers: *We must deal with this painful reality in Christian's lives!*

Within the church, there are almost as many divorced people as in the unbelieving and religious world. Should there not be clear, scriptural truths available and taught, which would alleviate much of the offences and pain caused by this human travesty?

We the ministry must study this topic, then act, taking responsibility for what we find in God's Word. If we genuinely love God and love our neighbor, should we not do our godly all to minister to these vast numbers of wounded souls? A horrible wrong and pain is perpetrated when we do not uphold godly standards with a sure knowledge. We would all weep if we only understood the effect caused by a wrongful lack in dealing with this subject. I believe heaven does.

Moses' Example

A great wrong is perpetrated on the believer because very few follow what Moses did with a heart for the church in the wilderness, when Israel was traveling to the promised land (Exodus 18:13, Acts 7:38). Moses spent entire days resolving people's problems. In time he corrected and improved his actions by setting a large number of elders in place to deal with the people problems in practical ways (Exodus 18:14).

Have people or God changed? Why are we not dealing with our believing people's problems in depth? Moses wound up speaking to God face-to-face, as a man speaks with a friend.

PERVERSION OF JUSTICE IN DIVORCE

Ungodly Bondage, Unbiblical Wrong

Why should my life be ruined due to another person's actions or wrongful inactions? Is there no justice from God's throne? Yes, there is. Our God is just and holy. He judges righteously in the affairs of men. He set righteous elders and kings in place with His holy directions as to how people were to be governed. King Jehoshaphat was a great example of a godly king, who by holy direction governed the people of Israel, as we should govern today,

> And Jehoshaphat dwelt at Jerusalem: and he went out again through the people from Beersheba to mount Ephraim, and brought them back unto the LORD God of their fathers. And he set judges in the land throughout all the fenced cities of Judah, city by city, *And said to the judges, Take heed what ye do: for ye judge not for man, but for the LORD, who is with you in the judgment.* Wherefore now let the fear of the LORD be upon you; take heed and do it: for there is no iniquity with the LORD our God, nor respect of persons, nor taking of gifts. Moreover in Jerusalem did Jehoshaphat

set of the Levites, and of the priests, and of the chief of the fathers of Israel, for the judgment of the LORD, and for controversies, when they returned to Jerusalem. And he charged them, saying, Thus shall ye do in the fear of the, faithfully, and with a perfect heart. And what so ever cause shall come to you of your brethren that dwell in their cities, between blood and blood, between law and commandment, statutes and judgments, ye shall even warn them that they trespass not against the LORD, and so wrath come upon you, and upon your brethren: this do, and ye shall not trespass.

2 Chronicles 19:4

The directions were clear, to judge righteously in controversy by setting up convenient holy courts to deal with difficult issues between God's people. God's people today are still God's people. He has not changed. He has set out His truths for man to follow and many of these have been ignored. Most churches and clergy are limited due to a lack of knowledge about this topic. Our God is righteous and holy. What man does with His truths by ignorance or intent is another matter. This especially applies to some religious denominations with a hard, loveless, and imbalanced understanding of God's loving and fair dealings regarding this most important and timely topic. We must know the whole council of God and have a balanced knowledge from the entire Bible, not selecting a limited few scriptures. We must get involved and deal with marriage difficulties with justice for all.

An Unrighteous God Portrayal

Many portray our Holy God as an unrighteous being, imposing laws of bondage, chains of limitations and wrong upon victims of an abusive marriage. Our God is the judge of all the earth and always does right, as proven to Abraham (Ge. 18:25). God removed the righteous before throwing brimstone on Sodom. Our God always sets a righteous judgment system in place, as we should be doing in the church. Then our people could take problems "to the church" (Mt. 18:17). Weigh God's directive to Moses:

> If a false witness rise up against any man to testify against him that which is wrong; Then both the men, between whom the controversy is, shall stand before the Lord, before the priests and the judges, which shall be in those days; And the judges shall make diligent inquisition: and, behold, if the witness be a false witness, and hath testified falsely against his brother; Then shall ye do unto him, as he had thought to have done unto his brother: so shalt thou put the evil away from among you.
>
> Deuteronomy 19:16

We experience a wrong portrayal of God's righteousness and teachings of same, when pulpits by their silence teach that a person locked into abuse and wrong has no availability of righteous remedies. Ultimately divorce may be one of these righteous remedies available. Our God never intended the marriage covenant to create an imprisonment where wrongful abuse must be tolerated. He is just, holy,

and righteous! It is man who, in sin and ignorance, perpe-
trates and justifies wrong. What kind of God are you and
I portraying?

Horrible, Ungodly Wrong
and Abuse of Authority

In the Philippines and other countries, we see a good
example of unrighteous wrong. The effect is so ugly and
damaging. There is no legal divorce legislation in place.
The lower house of government has passed a legislation
allowing for divorce under approved legislation laws. This
would and should become law after passage by the Senate.
However, at this writing it is held up, due to this being
stopped and challenged by the Roman Catholic Church.
All that exists is a Catholic Church-controlled government annulment. The effects are as follows:

1. An annulment, costing a huge amount of pesos in this
    impoverished nation, is only available to the wealthy.
    The cost is two to three years average wages.

2. The faithful and godly wife, who has a womanizing
    husband, is locked into a life of torment. She cannot
    divorce and find a genuine God-intended, loving hus-
    band. She is robbed of physical and emotional love,
    knowing he sleeps around. There is no alimony and
    child care involved, so she suffers through hoping for
    some help with the children's needs. His infidelity
    has shattered her hopes of a loving home with a life
    of married bliss, and she is bound to this mess for a

lifetime. The same applies to him when the wife is unfaithful.

3. The result is many of the more prominent men have mistresses elsewhere. Many children have no true father, as his attention is divided into more than one home.

4. If she leaves and moves in with another man, she is labeled as an adulterous person and lives under a cloud. Heartache, pain, and a wrongful stigma shroud her life. Many are legislated into a horrible injustice, due to unrighteous non-biblical untruth being enforced.

5. The Catholic Church prospers, regardless of the pain inflicted, while they wield chains of bondage with an unrighteous, unholy, wrongful authority.

6. An annulment states the initial marriage was in error, regardless of the effects on the children produced by this union. The church takes no responsibility in the error. The hell on earth and the damage to the people is comparable to any form of physical torture. Yet I believe much of this is practiced by ignorance, not knowing the God and Father of our LORD Jesus Christ or His ways.

The Painful Struggle

A godly wife or husband is living in a painful marriage, not knowing what to do. They are bound by their intentions to please God and believe that divorce is not an option under any circumstances. Or they may believe that one must gather sure and physical proof of one's spouse committing adultery to get out of the wrongs being perpetrated, which is almost impossible to obtain. Detectives and the time to catch and document a wily, cheating spouse are expensive and difficult.

Limited Knowledge

Due to a limited knowledge and untruth, being presented as to scriptural realities, the horrible results are:

1. A slow and painful death with no hope of genuine love.

2. A frustrated relationship while being imprisoned by a godly conscience wanting to do right, but lacking knowledge of God's remedies.

3. The spouse is involved with "X-rated" materials or pornography, killing a loving bedroom or being forced to accept a lustful relationship. There is an inability to be a genuine husband or wife in conjugal family relationships, with an unwillingness to discuss or attend counseling.

4. Abuse is being perpetrated verbally, or in one of the many forms this can take place.

5. The death of a love relationship is in progress. Perhaps this is due to a constant bombardment of destructive anger. This may not be obvious to others, being carefully concealed by a spouse. This destructive anger is attended with an unwillingness to attend counseling

to address this negative behavior. or an unwilling-ness on the part of a spouse to attend counseling and address problems.

6. Perhaps the problems within the relationship are agitated due to financial difficulties involving negative expenditures, with an unwillingness to discuss this topic with a gentle mutual accountability.

7. The children are always the victims of a wrongful relationship, suffering from wrong role models and parental neglect. Often, a false guilt of involvement affects them for their entire future lives and their marriages.

8. The whole family suffers.

God wants and demands genuine relationships involving His children and Him in heaven. He also expects us to build and retain genuine love relationships toward each other. Love God and your neighbor is the summarization of all laws. When this is not the case, the effect is a living death. The lack of and death of a genuine love expression is demonstrated from the following behavior:

1. When the husband is always staring at the slim and trim opposite sex outside of the marriage, he robs the wife of the single eyed focused love she deserves and needs.

2. The wife may or may not be aggressive in pursuing extramarital relationships, but she is gaining a library of *Harlequin Romance* books, or similar materials. For some wives it is living out a romance on afternoon TV

shows. Meanwhile their emotions and love disappear into the hero of the dream world, while the husband is robbed of their needed and expressed love required to maintain a healthy marriage. In any case, the focus is not on creating a loving home every husband deserves. This is applicable to both the husband and wife.

3. Supposedly godly people in church, not focusing their love toward the marriage partner. Some spend hours on internet relationships, living in a planned or unplanned eventual disaster.

4. The husband using his work as an escape is common, when unresolved relational difficulties exist. Meanwhile the wife is deprived of companionship and is exiled to a life of loneliness. When there is no time expenditure balance initiated, considering work, sports, and family pursuits, why wonder what went wrong when blindsided by a spouse's affair or demand for a divorce?

Who was the real guilty party in this marriage failure? Did both share in the guilt?

Marriage can be compared to a garden. Since we are all imperfect people with sin issues (pride, selfishness, impatience, attitudes, etc.), weeds will grow and pop up uninvited. When we do not deal with the weeds, they will overtake our garden. A few years ago, both my wife and I were determined to plant a vegetable and flower garden. The rhubarb always survived. Eventually the rest was completely overtaken by weeds since we just did not have the time to nurture and maintain this dream. We finally had a machine remove the entire evidence of our failed effort.

Most marriages are just like that. We must deal with the "weeds" that pop up. When you see sweet, successful marriages, be assured that they belong to experienced weeding teams. Those involved will have learned to honestly discuss, listen, act, and forgive with each other, always seeking the spouse's well-being.

Also, with a genuine love, they will act out what the apostle Peter said: "Love covers a multitude of sins" (1 Peter 4:8). We must be godly in all relationships, especially marriage, where love is the bonding adhesive holding the family together. Let's not be majoring on the minors when dealing with a spouse. May we honor and encourage, strengthen and uphold, "to have and to hold till death do us part" as much as possibly lies within us. We must know how to address wrongs in a godly manner.

Wrong mental prisons and bondages are common with huge numbers of Christian marriages, due to a lack of clear knowledge as to how they should be dealing with their relationship problems. A good example of bondage being perpetrated is when we consider the unbiblical error expressed by some religious groups. Lacking knowledge always verifies what the Bible expresses by God's prophet Hosea, "My people are destroyed for lack of knowledge" (Hosea 4:6)

When one considers an example of wrongful mental chains being imposed on people, consider the Mormons who have renamed themselves "The Church of The Latter

Day Saints." This fast-growing "cult" are a people in bondage, constantly pulling new proselytes into their bondage.

The true church denies them a genuine Christian standing because they deny two of the basic foundational doctrines of the true church (same as Jehovah Witnesses and other cults). They deny the deity of Christ, meaning that Christ was genuinely the only one God and "very God" when he was on earth, having humbled himself to take the form of man for the death on the cross. Christ was not just a prophet or Michael the archangel. Secondly, they deny the foundational doctrine of eternal judgment which the true church believes in. True believers deny the lie of annihilation.

Consider the atrocious mind bondage this cult places upon women who are deceived to believe that unless they "no matter what" are pleasing in servitude to their husbands, they will lose out on eternal future benefits in the afterlife. They teach that husbands will become gods of their own planets and the wives will be the mothering populating entities, but only at their husband's discretion. What an atrocious mental chain of putrid mind control is imposed on these women.

Instead of what they teach, what a glorious liberty Christ has given women, "There is neither Jew nor Greek, there is neither bond nor free, there is neither male nor female: for ye are all one in Christ Jesus" (Galatians 3:28).

We are so blessed to know that the genuine saved Christian shall stand at the merciful throne of Christ, who will judge us in righteousness (2 Corinthians 5:10). We know the power of His atonement and blood (1 John 1:9).

We believe in His promise of sins forgiven (John 5:24). Knowing the Bible truths regarding our position in Christ, sets a woman free from such bondage. Likewise, when one knows their scriptural rights and how to resolve problems with an assurance of heart due to knowing scriptural truth, they are blessed. The truth always sets one free (John 8:32).

Lack of Knowledge Ministers Death

We need clear and completely balanced knowledge to minister to our people as God set out in His Word by Malachi 2:7: "For the priest's lips should keep knowledge, and they should seek the law at his mouth: for he is the messenger of the LORD of hosts."

Due to a lack of knowledge, many divorced people suffer needlessly. They suffer within their inner being as wrongful pain is heaped on them by uninformed fellow believers as well as preachers. Out of a godly love for our wounded brethren, may we become knowledgeable as to the Bible truths involved which affect these believers. Again, in Hosea 6:4, the prophet states, "My people are destroyed for lack of knowledge."

This definitely applies in this topic, if we are to factually address Christ's summarization of the laws of God, to love God and our neighbor as ourselves (Matthew 22:37–39). We must study all of the biblically set out truths involved, to enable us to minister holy grace and truthful righteousness to the wounded casualties of this deadly minefield of human trauma. Most divorce casualties are victims, due to a very limited knowledge and help from others. Many are waiting for the truth and a clearly set out knowledge about this very topic.

My wife with her first husband, an American service man, while both of them were unsaved, came to the USA from the Philippines. Shortly thereafter he took other blonde interests, leaving her stranded. In the aftermath of the divorce, she got saved due to the ministry of a friend, Cathy Engel, while attending a Women's Aglow Fellowship meeting. Later she attended a large, full gospel church, where the preacher sent her home devastated. He taught that she would be committing adultery if she remarried. She was victimized by his adultery. The unjust mental chains wrongly imposed are not limited to cult groups. Good churches can also have wrong doctrines due to a lack of knowledge. Many well-meaning pulpits in ignorance preach chains of bondage. Yes, we find Christ's words where we are told that when a person breaks the marriage covenant and commits adultery, they are in sin. That is not at the expense of other Bible truths, regarding how we deal with controversy and marriage problems. Setting people free with a true knowledge by God's Word is part of what the Bible calls the "true fast."

True Fasting and Worship:

Christian fasting involves an intense time of seeking God. For those who practice fasting as a spiritual pursuit to worship seeking the LORD, consider what God calls "His chosen fast," spoken of in Isaiah. "Is not this the fast that I have chosen: to loose the bonds of wickedness, to undo the bands of the yoke, and to let the oppressed go free, and that ye break every yoke?" (Isaiah 58:6).

This fast had nothing to do with suppression of eating. This was a fast of time and heart dedication ministering to people's wounds. Are we prepared to "loose bonds of wickedness"? Are we prepared to "break yokes and set the oppressed free"? We should not require submission of our people to our spiritual authority or demand recognition of our leadership, unless we are prepared to take responsibility for them as we apply these scriptures and set captives free. We must confront and deal with heavy yokes and bondages.

Dealing with family problems, and especially divorce-related issues, is lifting yokes and bondages. All too often this topic has oppression, blindness, and ungodliness involved.
When we initiate a caring and holy dealing with our people, we will minister to and bring healing to numerous burdened hearts. May we study this matter scripturally, then act accordingly to our studied findings.

SCRIPTURAL DIVORCE: FIRST JUSTIFICATION

Some churches present a theology that divorce is not an option and not available for any reason for the genuinely "saved and born again" believers. Those churches have a zero tolerance for divorce. This is unbiblical.

Other so-called churches will allow divorce for any reason, including "she burned my toast," as well as same-sex marriages, even though both of these views are scripturally in error according to our holy God. The truth is, there are two scriptural and righteous divorce justifications for the genuine believer.

Justification Number One: Adultery

The first and most accepted reason within some churches, yet rarely dealt with correctly, is adultery. The Bible and our God Himself states divorce is acceptable when adultery is involved. Jesus Christ said in Matthew 19:9, And I say unto you, Whosoever shall put away his wife, except it be for fornication, and shall marry commits adultery: and whoso marries her which is put away doth commit adultery.

The Greek word for fornication is *porneia*. In the Strong's Concordance, this is defined as harlotry, adultery, incest, idolatry. Our LORD Jesus in this text clearly states that divorce is acceptable and allowed when a marriage partner is the victim of an adulterous partner. Those who ignore this "except" word by their logic or unbelief, deny God's Holy Word, ministering death to all those affected by their wrongful and sinful denial of God's Word.

When speaking of physical adultery, the scriptures are clear as to what is involved. This act of committing physical adultery breaks the "one flesh" covenant. To the married, our LORD said, "Wherefore they are no more twain, but one flesh. What therefore God hath joined together, let not man put asunder (Matthew 19:6)."

In adultery, a person leaves the "one flesh" covenant and joins him or herself to other flesh. In 1 Corinthians 6:15–19, the apostle Paul said:

> Know ye not that your bodies are the members of Christ? Shall I then take the members of Christ, and make them the members of a harlot? God forbid. What? Know ye not that he which is joined to a harlot is one body? For two, says he, shall be one flesh. But he that is joined unto the LORD is one spirit. Flee fornication. Every sin that a man does is without the body; but he that commits fornication sins against his own body. What? Know ye not that your body is the temple of the Holy Ghost which is in you, which ye have of God, and ye are not your own?
>
> Matthew 5:32

Except is also rendered as "saving for the cause of." The Greek word for this is *par-ek-tos.'* This is interpreted as G3844 and G1622; *near outside,* that is, *besides:* - except. This exception clearly states divorce is allowed for adultery. Under this exception, when one of the marriage partners who at the marriage altar promised to become one flesh with their spouse, breaks this covenant by committing adultery, they have broken their marriage covenant. The act of fornication gives clear justification for divorce to the innocent party.

This is not a law that says one must divorce, but it states one may divorce, per the words of our LORD Jesus Christ, the LORD of the Church. Unfortunately many disregard this Bible text.

Others destroy this text by adding to this scripture. They add man's reasoning, adding to and altering God's Word. Some will say, "Yes, divorce is permissible, however…" The added "however" can bring an unscriptural burden and bondage depending on what the "however" involves. They deteriorate Christ's words when they usually add, "It is better to forgive and stay in the relationship as this would be more pleasing to God."

Yes! The offended and innocent party may forgive if they so choose. However, to add the opinion of "However it is better…" is beyond what Jesus said. They add this due to their opinion as to Bible teachings about forgiveness.

Sin Has Results Besides
Needing Forgiveness

The Bible clearly teaches us to forgive each other in regards to confessed sins. Our Lord Jesus in Luke 17:3 taught, "Take heed to yourselves: If thy brother trespasses against thee, rebuke him; and if he repent, forgive him." Note that this forgiveness is subject to genuine repentance being expressed. God Himself will not forgive sins without repentance being involved.

The doctrine regarding repentance of sin is the first Bible doctrine of the six foundational Bible doctrines listed in Hebrews 6:1–2. Forgiveness does not automatically mean that relationships afterward go back to the same position as before a wrong was committed. Some will immediately say, "Well, if there is true forgiveness, should there not be a forgetting of the past fault and things go on as before the fault, with a continuing in the marriage?" Wrong! David was confronted by the prophet, Nathan, regarding sin and wrong involving Bathsheba and Uriah. Read God's holy justice and judgment with David's sin of adultery, which was followed by David's repentance and forgiveness (2 Samuel 11:2- 12:1–10–13). The Lord said you are forgiven, but "the sword shall not depart from your house."

Our holy God forgave David, but the results of his sin remained. In time he saw and experienced the prophesied sword from within his house, bringing destruction. Absalom, his son, attempted to kill David and forcefully take his throne. David became the man after God's heart, but experienced this bitter "sword" from within his own family when Absalom attempted to murder him and take the kingdom away by insurrection. This was a direct judgment and result from sins committed, although forgiven. God did not spare him from this regardless of David's strong repentance as we read from Psalm fifty-one (2 Samuel 15:12).

One should always forgive sin when genuinely repented of. However, this does not necessarily bring healing or trust to a broken marriage covenant. The decision to resume a marriage walk is left to the injured party. Forgiveness may still be attended with negative results due to the offense committed. Deny this truth and you are accusing our God of being unrighteous in His dealings with David and his adultery.

The results from this sin brought huge negative sorrows to David in his future years, regardless of God's stated forgiveness. This judgment was a direct result of the now forgiven sin. This reality ties into the truth Paul spoke of in Galatians 6:7, "Be not deceived; God is not mocked: for whatsoever a man sows, that shall he also reap."

Also, apostle Paul taught that sometimes you do not forgive people's sins until the person involved addresses the sin committed, demonstrating true repentance. As an example consider, "Now I beseech you, brethren, mark them which cause divisions and offences contrary to the doctrine which ye have learned; and avoid them" (Romans 16:17). This marking includes "no forgiveness" and avoidance until the sin is addressed and repented of.

Also our LORD said to the "born of the Spirit" believers when he breathed on them after rising from the dead, "And when he had said this, he breathed on them, and said unto them, Receive ye the Holy Ghost: Whosoever sins ye remit, they are remitted unto them; and whosoever sins ye retain, they are retained" (John 20:22). We the church must understand which sins are to be retained from those which are to be forgiven. Few relate to these scriptures. Have you heard a sermon about retaining sin lately? The sermon should start with "God retains sin," until it is repented of. Part of the substantiation for this fact is, "He that believeth on the Son hath everlasting life: and he that believeth not the Son shall not see life; but the wrath of God abides on him" (Jn. 3:36).

Stick to the Accurate Word

To add "It is better and more God-pleasing to forgive and to continue in the broken marriage" is not presenting a person's biblical rights. It adds an opinion of questionable wisdom. It brings a dimension of mental bondage to the innocent party, when we add "it is better to stay in the marriage," when infidelity has been perpetrated. Regarding forgiveness, the correct manner of stating the truth to the innocent victim of an adulterous partner, when adultery is involved should be as follows:

Yes, as hard as it may be, you should forgive the transgressing partner *when* they truly repent. This does not affect your right to divorce the husband or wife who broke the "one flesh covenant." You alone have the choice and complete right to either divorce the guilty partner or work toward reconciliation. You should forgive them if they repent, but you still have the right to a scriptural divorce. The choice is completely yours to make. The Bible allows you the freedom to make the decision either way.

The Holy Word is clear about this: "And I say unto you, Whosoever shall put away his wife, except for fornication…" (Matthew 19:9).

Our LORD Jesus sets the injured party free while some will hold them by imposing a false guilt and bondage. The clear truth is that just because one should forgive does not mean they need to continue in the broken marriage. Who but the affected and betrayed marriage partner knows the dimension of pain brought to the victim of the marriage betrayal?

Who but the person involved can know whether or not they can again face the risk of trusting the one who betrayed their marriage covenant? Set people free under God without manipulating their rights. Teach them how to handle this and, in the case of someone forgiving the adulterous spouse, teach them to not use this past sin as a club after having "forgiven."

I will never forget my pastoral life experience while ministering to a dedicated, attractive Christian lady from British Columbia, Canada. She was suicidal after catching her husband in a second adulterous affair which was hidden to others, and I knew due to being her pastor. She forgave the first occasion, even though suspecting there were more adulterous occasions involved.

She was stopped while in the very act of committing suicide, God being gracious to her as someone intervened. She was so disturbed that she pleaded with the intervening person not to stop her suicidal effort of swallowing a quantity of a deadly substance. Her painful story was that she had been advised by a past counselor that it would be "more God-pleasing" to forgive the adulterous husband and reconcile.

Wanting to be "more God-pleasing," this wrongly informed quality saint worked toward forgiveness while being in her early twenties, following the first betrayal. The marriage was never "right" and now years later, she could not face the continual multiple betrayals and the lost years. She sadly said, "I should have divorced him and married an eligible person, as I knew this was available to me. Instead, I listened to the counsel of "Staying in the marriage is a God-pleasing, better way," which, in fact, was a "worse" way. As of that day, I personally will not add a "better way."

I might advise that forgiveness is a mandatory need, should genuine repentance be evidenced. However, to divorce or not to divorce is solely their choice. Our LORD did not add the words "it is better" to do this or that; however, He did state we must forgive the repenting offender.

God Hates Divorce

God hates divorce. He only allows this when righteously inevitable. The Word of God calls marriage a covenant. In Malachi 2:16, "For I hate divorce, says the LORD, and him who covers his garment (his clothing, what he wears) with wrong." Having said that, God accepts divorce as an undesirable solution when He determines that no other just solution is available.

Our Lord said, "And I say unto you, Whosoever shall put away his wife, except for fornication" (Matthew 19:9). God righteously allows this divorce judgment, based on a person's actions. God decrees a righteous judgment in all things according to our actions. If we do not sow, do not expect to reap. If we do not forgive, do not expect to receive personal forgiveness.

God Himself will enter into divorce over wrongdoing, with a broken heart. He always longs for true love and unity with restoration. He sent His Son to the cross for this purpose. His will is that none should perish, but sadly millions will (2 Peter 3:9). If we do not see this statement as sound scriptural theology, we will not be capable of calling any divorce righteous. Neither will we be equipped to properly deal with this topic in people's lives. We must study and know the "whole counsel of the Word of God," regarding this major and important topic affecting so many.

Does God Divorce Himself from People?

Yes! "And I said after she had done all these things, Turn thou unto me. But she returned not. And her treacherous sister Judah saw it. And I saw, when for all the causes whereby backsliding Israel committed adultery I had put her away, and given her a bill of divorce" (Jeremiah 3:7–8). The prophet is speaking about God divorcing Israel. Read it in context! He does not say chasten, or separating Himself from them, but divorcement! A Bill of Divorce is a legal memorialized document, attesting to the past covenanted relationship being dissolved. (Many have them court issued).

God is Holy and Righteous and is so named. Our God is a god of covenant and when one gets saved, God enters into a covenant with that person. God made covenant with Israel. This covenant was limited and only applied to those who obeyed Him in circumcision and the keeping of His laws, believing in Him and wholeheartedly seeking after Him (Genesis 17:7, 11–14, 19).

Israel broke God's covenant terms. The God of Israel was grieved by the actions of Israel, discerning their evilheartedness and judging them due to the betrayal of their covenant relationship. He divorced them and caused Jeremiah to write about this. God lamented with words of pain by Jeremiah: "For my people have committed two evils; they have forsaken me the fountain of living waters…" (Jeremiah 2:13)

The result of this judgment due to their actions was seen when Israel was overpowered by the Babylonian king, with many being slaughtered. Those who did not escape, men, women, and children were all trooped as a herd of naked cattle and marched into Babylon for seventy years, including Daniel (Ezekiel 16:38–43, 23:25–30).

Our God said, "And I saw all the causes by which Israel committed adultery" (Jeremiah 3:8). He finally gave

Israel a bill of divorcement. Isaiah writes about all the causes our God spoke of in Isaiah 57:5: "Enflaming yourselves with idols under every green tree, slaying the children in the valleys under the clefts of the rocks"? Many in Israel eventually killed their children in sacrifice to Baal and forced their children to walk through fire to the idol Moloch. God esteems idolatry as adultery, besides making a covenant with evil.

Our God again explains why He gave Israel a bill of divorcement. In Jeremiah 3:6–13 the prophet, Jeremiah, expressed the wounded heart of God under holy anointing, "Oh that my head were waters, and mine eyes a fountain of tears, that I might weep day and night for the slain of the daughter of my people" (Jeremiah 9:1)!

God pronounced His judgment over them due to their actions, as prophesied by His prophet Ezekiel:

> Wherefore I poured my fury upon them for the blood that they had shed upon the land, and for their idols wherewith they had polluted it: And I scattered them among the heathen, and they were dispersed through the countries: according to their way and according to their doings I judged them.
>
> Ezekiel 36:18–19

This scattering did not take place until AD 70, but was under an immovable decree of God when Ezekiel prophesied this. God judged and divorced them! We have seen this scattering judgment in effect for almost two thousand years, until they were gathered from the nations primarily due to Hitler, the "hunter," in World War Two (Jeremiah 16:15–16). They again became a nation in 1948.

Moses commanded the Israelites to give a bill of divorcement should there be displeasure and conflict in the marriage. "When a man hath taken a wife, and married her, and it come to pass that she find no favor in his eyes, because he hath found some uncleanness in her, then let him write her a bill of divorcement, and give it in her hand, and send her out of his house" (Deuteronomy 24:1). This was to finalize the documentation of the broken marriage, allowing the wife the freedom to remarry and not be left hanging with a cloud over her head. Moses did this out of a just mercy toward the estranged women.

CHURCH AND BELIEVER'S RESPONSIBILITIES

Divorce Justification Beyond Physical Adultery

The LORD holds all of us responsible for our actions and deals with us accordingly. This is evidenced by whether a person finds salvation or not. Only the seeking and willing people come to salvation in Christ, even though it is God's will that all mankind be saved. (Matthew 5:3–9, Revelations 22:17, 2 Peter 3:9) Our actions are weighed and determine our future: "Be not deceived; God is not mocked: for whatsoever a man sows, that shall he also reap" (Galatians 6:7). We must make decisions in all areas of life, and these decisions bear results. This truth applies to marital decisions as well, affecting the results of the relationship.

The second and more prevalent reason for divorce among believers is the result of ungodly actions within the marriage. When one or both of the marriage partners has chosen a path of unwillingness to deal with ungodly actions within the marriage, a potential divorce proceeding is on the horizon. An unwillingness to address and deal with painful issues at the request of a marriage partner places the marriage on a slippery slope.

The need of dealing with the actions of an ungodly marriage partner in a biblical fashion in these circumstances is of great importance. Often this does not happen and avoidable divorces take place. Here, the main fault lies with the ministry and church. This is due to the failure of not teaching godly directives to the flock regarding these matters.

Few churches promote that the membership should seek out the leadership to help resolve controversy and difficulties, including marriage problems. To sum this up, much of this is due to the ministry leadership not being scripturally knowledgeable, as many demonstrate their lack by not taking responsibility for membership relational difficulties.

The common church knowledge presentation is usually limited to physical adultery being the only "clouded" reason for a quasi-acceptable divorcing. This is accompanied with the clouded dubious right to remarry. God's banquet table of the many and balanced truths involving marriage, separation, divorce, and remarriage are rarely understood or presented.

Many lack the shepherd's heart required to get involved and care for the hurting in the flock. Few ministries seem to be willing to take this just responsibility. It seems that few will risk standing with the hurting by confronting wrong in the face of controversy.

True and mature ministry will hurt when the flock hurts and will weep with those who weep. An immature, doctrinally weak ministry will fail in handling their responsibility. This is verified by the fact that extremely few churches and ministries teach the believers what they should do when they run into relationship troubles they cannot resolve.

A believer, who is not accountable to a genuine godly leadership, is also responsible for the loss of this ministry protection. This should exist in all true believers' lives. Regardless of what the believer should do, a properly functioning church leadership should teach and know how to deal with people problems.

Jesus Christ's Instructions to Believers: Matthew Chapter Eighteen

Our Lord Jesus Christ gave clear instructions to all believers as to how knowledgeable and discerning believers should deal with relationship problems. In Matthew, the eighteenth chapter, we find God's clearly set out rules for dealing with problems. These instructions are just as relevant today as at the time when our Lord and Savior gave these, as He walked this earth teaching for three years. They are just as relevant as the key and pivotal scripture of John 3:3, where we are told a believer must be born again to enter the kingdom of God. Love desires to communicate, understand, and be understood.

In summary, the following three truths sadly apply:

1. For centuries, the majority of the Church has ignored their responsibility in applying these instructions.

2. They have not taught their adherents to follow these instructions.

3. Only a rare few churches exist which have the appropriate ministry people available to follow these instructions, not having a genuine, mature, multiple eldership.

The Church Should Be a Righteous Refuge for the Wounded

Jesus, the LORD of the Church, clearly taught in Matthew 18:15–18:

> Moreover if thy brother shall trespass against thee, go and tell him his fault between thee and him alone: if he shall hear thee, thou hast gained thy brother. But if he will not hear thee, then take with thee one or two more, that in the mouth of two or three witnesses every word may be established. And if he shall neglect to hear them, *tell it unto the church:* but if he neglects to hear the church, let him be unto thee as a heathen man and a publican. Verily I say unto you, Whatsoever ye shall bind on earth shall be bound in heaven: and whatsoever ye shall loose on earth shall be loosed in heaven.

The church needs to take its place and fulfill the duties outlined here by our LORD.

Communication between two married partners is vital. When this is gone, the marriage becomes a difficult existence with a "roommate" relationship. Other needs may still be addressed, but love and a heart-to-heart intimacy of relationship is damaged and sometimes beyond repair. We must prioritize peaceful and careful discussion in matters of the heart.

The rules of 1 Corinthians 13, addressing the genuine components of love, must be applied. Love is patient and is not easily provoked and given to anger. Love is desirous of walking in truth and righteous fairness. Love is not selfish; it believes and hopes for good toward others. Love wants to hear and understand. Love wants to bring healing to a struggling mate's heart. When this is not the case, the qualities of a loving godly Christian marriage are deteriorated to a convenience existence. Our Lord Jesus said, "Moreover if thy brother shall trespass against thee, go and tell him his fault between thee and him alone."

This is Christ's commandment to you and me. We are to make every possible effort to personally discuss matters. This precedes any discussion with others. This is love in action! Here we cross swords with Solomon's wise counsel, "He who covers a transgression seeks love, but he who repeats a matter separates friends" (Pro. 17:9). Indiscrete conversation will cause damage to any relationship. We must be patient and wise in our marital dealings. This especially applies to those seeking counsel from others. Carefully weigh who you choose to approach and what the limits of your conversation are. Stirring up a following of your personal well-wishers may prove to bring a death blow to your relationship with your spouse. "Go to the brother" is the directive. Exhaust this possibility before proceeding beyond this potential avenue of healing. Go in a godly manner with a godly attitude of love and care. Only when this is exhausted should you consider the next directive.

Our Second Instruction: Involve Others

Our LORD is very clear in communicating the second step if one cannot make headway with personal, gentle communications. Involve one or two other believers. This is the moment where the fruit of your life relationships is shown for what they are. May they be godly and mature believers who have a depth of holy knowledge to provide godly and mature counseling. Godly wisdom and insight are needed in these emotionally charged waters.

The road block to involving others may be that you and your partner do not have the people relationships which both of you trust to be of value for transparent, unbiased input. Here we see the importance of the quality and fruit from which our relationship gardens have been growing.

The more common problem is the unholy pride of an implacable marriage partner who has stubborn resistance to humbly asking for help. I know of one couple where the wife firmly stood on the statement and held the stance of "We do not need to share our laundry with others." Even when things got very rough, she would not budge from this stubborn, prideful stance. When things cannot be ironed out between marriage partners, we need to humbly involve others. This is critical to retaining and mending a torn relationship and is also practicing the keeping of the Christ commanded directive of "feed my lambs and sheep."

That marriage eventually ended. In a large measure, the end arrived due to this stance of the refusal to involve others. The key is opening communication to achieve unity by bridging differences of priorities and understandings. Counselors are of great value. When in trouble, it becomes very difficult to look beyond the trees of the forest we are lost in. Others may help us to see. Refusal to involve others, with an ungodly pride, often results with divorce papers being filed. We do not have the right to prevent the involvement of others when this is requested by a marriage partner. May both parties have a voice in the selection of who the "others" are, but we must humbly be open to the involvement of others.

Our Third Instruction:
Take It to the Church

We are clearly told by our Lord as to what we must do. First, patiently and lovingly discuss the issues involved, while practicing the art of patience while listening, which is half of communication, to resolve difficulties. If this does not achieve resolution of the issues involved, get some godly people involved to solve the problems. Should this not bring solutions attended with harmony and peace, take it to the church. "The church" means the governing multiple ministering eldership. These participating elders are meant to be mature men and women of God who understand the guidelines of 1 Timothy 3:1–9 and Titus 1:5–9, which establish maturity guidelines. These are those spiritually mature believers who in plurality should govern the affairs in all churches. These are appointed by the mature existing leadership and not voted in by an average vote of the congregation. We see the New Testament example of this as read from Acts 20:17, where Paul called for the plural elders of the Ephesians church to meet with him, "And from Miletus he sent to Ephesus, and called the elders of the church."

These mature elders met with Paul, coming in humility when requested. Paul described their elder/overseer responsibilities, which are included with their "elder" position: "Take heed therefore unto yourselves, and to all the flock, over which the Holy Ghost hath made you overseers, to feed the church of God, which he hath purchased with his own blood" (Acts 20:28). This taking oversight responsibility included caring for the needs of the believers. This included bringing resolution to personal people dealings and marriage conflicts. The church is lacking and out of order if they are not receptive to and desirous of resolving conflict.

Some will no doubt accuse me of being critical of "the church." No! I love the church for which Christ shed His blood. Because of this I write. The real church is not a denomination, but individual believers, of which many are wounded and hurting, including wounded elders and leadership ministry. A critical person only criticizes. A constructive critic provides answers with the criticism.

Let's face real facts. It is almost a nonexistent occurrence to hear of a person taking their problems to "the church." It is also almost nonexistent for the church to seriously hear a matter and see it through to the conclusion of the matter. This takes real heart and grit. The demonstrated lack is common when dealing with people's difficulties. One "pastor" I know told some people to just avoid each other and walk up a different aisle when you see them. Now, serve communion with this outlook.

Another preacher, held in esteem by a number of people I am acquainted with, spent time bridging difficulties between some people by enforcing forgiveness while ignoring matters of difficulty , a huge, missing ingredient needing to be addressed to bring resolution solution to conflict. One of the parties said I want peace and forgiveness but I vow to never talk about the issues involved. This stance was acceptable to the counseling "peace maker." Mature counseling will not allow this stance, but will pierce this hard boil to bring healing. The situation resulted in a cold war stance of words without substance or genuine healing.

Church Judgment and Heathen Declaration

This is an extremely important factor in the entire process and so neglected. Here the holy biblical words of Christ are 99 percent disregarded. The difference between the one who listens to godly input and counseling and the person who neglects holy directives greatly affects their position and treatment, should there be a dissolving of the marriage.

Our LORD Jesus said, "And if he shall neglect to hear them, tell it unto the church: but if he neglect to hear the church, let him be unto thee as a heathen man and a publican." This is critical to the obedient and willing believer as to their future marital rights. When we apply this truth of a commanded and God given declaration to the ungodly spouse, setting forth their position as an unbeliever rejected by the church, this greatly affects the marital position of the spouse deemed just. This enters into the teachings of marriage and separation or divorce that Apostle Paul wrote about in 1 Corinthians chapter seven. This speaks to the issue of whether a believer is living with another believer or an unbeliever. The manner in which one is submissive and whether one honors the church-called leadership with holy counsel, is tremendously important. May the called leadership be knowledgeable of their authority and responsibility while ministering in God's sight.

How rare is it to find a church which will hold both parties accountable for their words and actions, insisting upon the counseling given to be followed. It is even more unusual to find the church which will make a judgment, should they determine that one party will not apply godly remedies in the controversy.

Then it is almost nonexistent to find a church which will publicly declare a person who did not listen to the church to be considered as a heathen. Is this not the case?

Is this not because these scriptural directions are ignored? Usually there is no judging of sin and wrong with a pulpit upheld verdict as to wrong. Unrepentant wrong doers should be considered and declared to be "publican and heathens" (unbelievers), according to our LORD.

This statement and fact hugely affects the position of rights to the believer if the marriage fails.

Unfortunately, we have denied Christ's holy instructions to His called and placed government leadership. We often fail in placing and establishing His desired leadership. We greatly fail the believers and church when a multiple saved and mature eldership is not made available.

For those who judge the setting forth of this truth to be "legalistic" or too hard, you have the right to ignore God's directions and Word. That is a choice we all make. As for me and my house, we will serve the LORD. Obedience is better than sacrifice (religious appearances):

> And Samuel said, Hath the LORD as great delight in burnt offerings and sacrifices, as in obeying the voice of the LORD? Behold, to obey is better than sacrifice, and to hearken than the fat of rams. 23 For rebellion is as the sin of witchcraft, and stubbornness is as iniquity and idolatry. Because thou hast rejected the word of the LORD, he hath also rejected thee from being king.
>
> 1 Samuel 15:22

The genuine and godly church is to be the true believer's refuge for righteous defense and peace, including a righteously pronounced divorce when applicable. Yes, I know that Jesus said "blessed are the peace makers" (Matthew 5:9). We should always attempt to bridge differences and bring unity. I personally despise divorce, knowing what it does to all involved. There are many writings about divorce recovery and healing for the broken.

Knowledge of truth also promotes healing.

Let's consider the wrongs which potentially bring a divorce about and how we should deal with these, since many are denied a righteous divorce due to lacking knowledge. Are you brokenhearted? Are you struggling with ungodly wrong due to the words and deeds of an unrighteous mate? Are you suffering in a bondage situation where there are painful, invisible shackles binding you in the stranglehold of a wrongful relationship? If so, the Word of God directs you to take these three steps as directed in Matthew, chapter eighteen. Deny and disregard these steps, and one will have a difficult time attaining a peaceful life and ending to any marriage.

1. Talk to the offending person. Communicate your pain and struggles. While talking, know discussion includes listening and making an effort to understand the other party's thoughts. As well as having a right heart, be patient. Be willing to forgive wrong when admitted to and repented of. Allow some time in this process. Some issues take time to consider and digest, but also

discern avoidance and express your right to discussion and confronting wrong in painful matters. Know that we owe the marriage partner the time and care to hear and communicate with patient, loving dialogue. Only when this step is exhausted should we progress to the next instruction our LORD gave. When discussion between the two of you does not produce a "reasonable" resolution of the problems, follow the second step. One robs themselves of the rightful resolution to a bondage life when they disregard this scriptural directive. Or they voluntarily succumb to a wrongful, self-chosen prison of a painful existence.

2. Now attempt to include and discuss the struggle areas with other godly, mature believers being involved. This is your right and responsibility! Find two or three other appropriate people who can be involved in discussion with the offending mate. This is your Christ-given right. The intent is to bring about reconciliation and unity in the relationship. Be sensitive. Here, the biblical teaching of the apostle James should apply, "Wherefore, my beloved brethren, let every man be swift to hear, slow to speak, slow to wrath" (James 1:19). Now consider the *extreme importance* of having quality, godly, personal, Christian relationships. They will always attempt to be spiritual safety barricades on the dangerous roads of life, which are full of unexpected bends and twists.

Do not be "super-spiritual" deceiving one's self. Yes, it is good and correct to pray, read the Word, attend church, and follow godly pursuits, but remember our God's prioritizing genuine peace and harmony with brethren, including your spouse: "Therefore if you offer your gift on the altar, and there remember that your brother has anything against you, leave your gift there before the altar and go. First be reconciled to your brother, and then come and offer your gift" (Matthew 5:23). Our God places a higher priority on genuine peace and unity over religious worship.

Get rid of the prideful "I want to look perfect" stance before others while your marriage is dying. Attempt to peacefully discuss the offensive issues with love and patience. Allow the wisdom of those whom you have involved to be heard, as you prayerfully discuss the issues in depth. Do not give in to those who preach to "forgive and move on," which is a bandage solution when the surgery of dealing with the root issues is needed to bring healing.

Mature, helping "witnesses" will know that the discussions are private and will protect the contents from wrongful gossip. Are your Christian friends mature enough for such an occasion? Consider the application of God's Holy Word. If painful problems are resolved and a holy unity established, praise God! Allow time and patient, loving effort to do its work until this avenue is exhausted.

3. If it is clear that if there is no resolution to the difficulties under discussion and disunity remains, do what our LORD directed us to do: *Take it to the church!* If you do not take it to the church, you have failed your godly

duty and Christ's directions for dealing with problems with your spouse.

Should your marriage partner not allow discussion about the problems with others involved, take it directly to the church. The church must respond and face their godly responsibility. If they do not take you seriously, find a believing church that trembles at God's Word (Isaiah 66:2).

Get away from "Pharisees" who will not take responsibility with compassion for all involved. Many preach correctly and our LORD said for us to follow their preaching, but will they put intense loving action into your life beyond preaching words:

> "All therefore whatsoever they bid you observe, that observe and do; but do not ye after their works: for they say, and do not. For *they* bind heavy burdens and grievous to be borne, and lay them on men's shoulders; but they themselves will not move them with one of their fingers. But all their works they do for to be seen of men: they make broad their phylacteries, and enlarge the borders of their garments, And love the uppermost rooms at feasts, and the chief seats in the synagogues, And greetings in the markets, and to be called of men, Rabbi, Rabbi." (Reverend, Pastor).
>
> Matthew 23:3–7

Some wounded marriage partners will not address wrong since they want to protect children or they do not have better opportunities for a peaceful alternative after a divorce. The choice is solely yours. Only those directly involved know when to act and get church involvement. We must know our scriptural rights and directives as to conduct acceptable to God. Know this; one of these directives in marriage is that God has called us to live at peace. (1 Corinthians 7:15) We must know the principles of God directed conduct to be enabled to live at peace, including life within Christian marriages.

COVENANTS HAVE
CONDITIONS

Marriage Is a Covenant

The exchanging of marriage vows involves entering into a covenant before God. We swear to the conditions of that covenant.

There are also conditions to the covenant God makes with us who are saved, which we must keep. One of these conditions is found in Hebrews 12:14: "Follow peace with all men, and holiness, without which no man shall see the LORD." Saved and all, if we do not retain a holy walk, we will not see God in an eternal heaven. Also, Paul said, "Wherefore, my beloved, as ye have always obeyed, not as in my presence only, but now much more in my absence, work out your own salvation with fear and trembling" (Philippians 2:12).

Paul clearly set out our responsibility to seek the LORD while walking in righteous and holy behavior when he said, "Know ye not that the unrighteous shall not inherit the kingdom of God? Be not deceived: neither fornicators, nor idolaters, nor adulterers, nor effeminate (homosexuals), nor abusers of themselves with mankind" (1 Corinthians 6:9). This text does not say "except for born again believers," as some would like it to say.

These texts underscore our responsibilities in walking before God. My "dearly beloved" is addressed to the saved Philippians church and us as well. We need to work out our salvation.

God named Israel His covenant people, to them and us as well God's covenant making applies, "Who are Israelites; to whom belong the adoption, and the glory, and the covenants, and the giving of the law, and the service of God, and the promises." (Romans 9:4) These blessings and these promises are ours as well. Our covenant with God has not changed.

"If" Is a Conditional Word

One of the most important Words in the Bible is the word *if.* The if word states a choice has to be made, resulting in cause and effect. God's Word is full of if's. This applies to sowing and reaping. This applies to salvation or not. This applies to the welfare of our live's circumstances. Consider the ramifications of what Moses said and is still applicable to our lives today, "If my people, which are called by my name, shall humble themselves, and pray, and seek my face, and turn from their wicked ways; then will I hear from heaven, and will forgive their sin, and will heal their land." (2 Chronicles 7:14) This if word applied to our Bible example people of Israel. This if word affected their covenant status, and will affect our marriage covenant status as well.

God made a covenant with Israel and gave them the promises of covenant blessings and life. As well, He warned His covenant people of curses and death should they betray His covenant: "And it shall come to pass, *if* thou shalt hearken diligently unto the voice of Lord thy God, to observe and to do all his commandments which I command thee this day, that the Lord thy God will set thee on high above all nations of the earth: And all these blessings shall come on thee" (Deuteronomy 28:1–2).

Note that the promised blessings are based on "If," and are followed by the curses in verse fifteen: "But it shall come to pass, if (if) thou wilt not hearken unto the voice of the Lord thy God, to observe to do all his commandments and his statutes which I command thee this day; that all these curses shall come upon thee, and overtake thee."

These promised curses are as real as the potential blessings that were promised to the faithful in Israel. Note that the curses led to perishing, death, and separation from God, due to serving gods of wood and stone if they did not serve Jehovah God (Deuteronomy 28:15, 36, 64).

Their future and fate depended on their actions. Both the going into captivity as well as the scattering of Israel due to forsaking the Lord, as prophetically written, took place when they disregarded Moses' statements and forsook Jehovah their God. Moses spoke this possibility of being scattered to Israel as a warning to be chaste and faithful (Deuteronomy 28:64). This prophesy of being scattered among the nations happened due to the betrayal of breaking God's covenant and took place in AD 70 (Ezekiel

36:18). The prophesied re-gathering took place much later in 1940–45. In Jeremiah, God prophesied how the "hunter" would bring them back (Jeremiah 16:15–16).

History has confirmed this incomparable and prophesied dealing, experienced by the Jews as Hitler's Nazi regime hunted them from house to house throughout Europe, the Baltics, and the Russian fringe countries for five years. No other nationality was ever hunted among the nations nor maintained their identity while being scattered for 1900 years.

The "if" word is huge as to cause and effect. This same "if" applies to our marriage dealings as well. If we do not deal with and reason through marital difficulties, we harvest marital relationships which are far below what can be achieved and enjoyed.

God's Divorcing Israel

God divorced Israel! Yes, these were His covenant people. In Isaiah 49:26–50:1, God states:

> "I the LORD am thy Savior and thy Redeemer, the mighty One of Jacob. Thus saith the LORD, Where is the bill of your mother's divorcement, whom I have put away? Or which of my creditors is it to which I have sold you? Behold, for your iniquities have ye sold yourselves, and for your transgressions is your mother put away."

This explains *God's divorcement of covenant people,* covenant people and all.

If our God, after making this statement, did not divorce Israel, He would be guilty of foolish talk. If we ignore and deny these statements, then we are guilty of a foolish disregard of His Word.

Our LORD God brought this subject up and had this written in His holy Word. If this possibility was not a reality, then why would He have said this? The LORD and Redeemer of Jacob divorced Israel because of their actions. Yet He was faithful to the remnant who sought Him, as Daniel did in the captivity to Babylon. Even before and after the scattering in AD 70, the Jews who accepted Jesus as the Messiah became Christians. The rest have denied Christ even until today.

The basis of God divorcing believers and covenant people is that He judges the reality of them having forsaken His covenant and acknowledging what people do. The reality of God separating Himself and denying His covenant people due to inaction of what He rightfully requires is seen from His stringent laws regarding circumcision.

The same truth basis applies to marriage. When scriptural rights and responsibilities are ignored, the door to an eventual divorce is ajar. As such let us examine this scriptural example involving circumcision, since the results of ignoring this scriptural principle were so severe.

Circumcision

Circumcision was a demand God placed upon man. Should this demand not be kept and followed per God's demand,

God stated that the offending person was not party to His covenant: "And the uncircumcised man child whose flesh of his foreskin is not circumcised, that soul shall be cut off from his people; he hath broken my covenant" (Genesis 17:14). Note that man can break God's covenant. Note the result is the covenant breaker is no longer a party to God's covenant.

God recognizes that covenants can be broken and the same covenant breaking possibility applies to marriage, which is also a covenant.

Since the covenant making was accompanied by a demand to circumcise every male child, perhaps we should consider the meaning of this demanded dealing, especially when God states that the uncircumcised male has broken His covenant (Genesis 17:11–14). Circumcision has several parts to this rite for us to understand.

The first truth depicted is that it is a sign "between me and you" (Genesis 17:11). It is a daily reminder and a hidden token which our God always sees, and is not visible to others. Our true heart covenant is and should be likewise and only the fruit of this covenant should be visible.

The male part that is involved is not simply needed for passing urine (consider female). It is the instrument of sowing. It speaks of our works and what we produce. Circumcision speaks of unsheathed, uncloaked, transparent sowing. This speaks of creating the fruit of a transparent holy heritage and lineage. It speaks of walking before God, being visible to Him and uncloaked in all of our doings and works.

May we remember this when we consider our covenant in marriage dealings between a man and woman. Our God does.

God Divorced Covenant Breakers

God accused Israel of having broken His covenant with Him.

> And the LORD said unto me, A conspiracy is found among the men of Judah, and among the inhabitants of Jerusalem. They are turned back to the iniquities of their forefathers, which refused to hear my words; and they went after other gods to serve them: the house of Israel and the house of Judah have broken my covenant, which I made with their fathers. Therefore thus says the LORD, Behold, I will bring evil upon them, which they shall not be able to escape; and though they shall cry unto me, I will not hearken unto them.
>
> Jeremiah 11:9–11

Consider the horrible death and atrocities in the AD 70 scattering and the 1940–45 holocaust gathering. Consider the huge genocide perpetrated when the Roman Empire general Titus, with his vast army, burned Jerusalem, destroyed the temple, and killed as many Jews as he could find. Now, tell me these people who our God destroyed in judgment will be saved and in heaven?

This is a vastly different picture from the portrayal to faithful believers—"He that dwells in the secret place of the most High, shall abide under the shadow of the Almighty. I will say of the LORD, He is my refuge and my fortress" (Psalm 91:1–2).

God drove the Jews to other nations and away from the Jerusalem center of worship, where they were set free to serve other gods,

> "Even all nations shall say, Wherefore hath the LORD done thus unto this land? What means the heat of this great anger? Then men shall say, Because *they have forsaken the covenant of the LORD* God of their fathers, which he made with them when he brought them forth out of the land of Egypt: For they went and served other gods, and worshipped them, gods whom they knew not, and whom he had not given unto them: And the anger of the LORD was kindled against this land, to bring upon it all the curses that are written in this book: And the LORD rooted them out of their land in anger, and in wrath, and in great indignation, and cast them into another land, as it is this day."
>
> Deuteronomy 29:24–28

God divorced Himself from covenant people. Marriage covenants can also end with a righteous divorcement. Do not be so foolish and believe these divorced people are saved and will inherit heaven. God made a covenant with these people, and because "his people *have forsaken the covenant of the LORD God of their fathers,*" he divorced them.

Do not be so foolish as to think that these Jews who worshipped other gods, and who Paul declares as "blind," circumcised, and all will be saved. God divorced them! God Himself will divorce covenant breakers! He swore to them:

> "When your fathers tempted me, proved me, and saw my works forty years. Wherefore I was grieved with that generation, and said, They do always err in their heart; and they have not known my ways. So I swore in my wrath, They shall not enter into my rest. Take heed, brethren, lest there be in any of you an evil heart of unbelief, in departing from the living God. But exhort one another daily, while it is called To day; lest any of you be hardened through the deceitfulness of sin. For we are made partakers of Christ, if we hold the beginning of our confidence steadfast unto the end."

> Hebrews 3:9

God swore that these Israelites would never enter into His rest. He also showed His disdain for them, stating their "carcasses" were strewn throughout the desert. We, as well as them, enter in due to steadfast faith until the end. Our God swore that these Israelites would not enter into His rest due to their unbelief (Hebrews 3:18–19).

Basis for God's Divorcing Man

If you believe that God never separates Himself from any covenant Israelite, the forgoing writings of textual truths are lost on you. When it comes to Bible doctrine and truth, someone once said, "It is easy to break a stick, but a bundle of sticks is difficult to break." Likewise, the bundle of sticks of truth regarding this subject could be listed on thirty pages of writings and is impossible to break. Our God does not and has not changed. He is not a respecter of persons. The same principles apply when God departs from and brings judgment upon New Testament covenant believers!

God's Spirit departed from Adam and Eve in the day they chose to betray God, due to entering into sin. They died a spiritual death just as our God said they would. Before they sinned, God's Spirit was joined to their spirit. They spiritually died due to being spiritually separated from the living God. Only due to their faith in the Messiah to come, and what Christ the Messiah would do, were their lives restored. The same temptations apply to Christians today. We choose in all matters, including salvation and whether to live in holiness.

Do not think the born again believer cannot come to a place of being "twice dead" (Jude 1:12). Paul said and warned the believing Christian women, "Now she that is a widow indeed, and desolate, trusts in God, and continues in supplications and prayers night and day. But she that lives in pleasure is dead while she lives" (1 Timothy 5:5). This was written to the church believers right after directions to elder men, women, sisters, and widows about living a Godly lifestyle. God's only words to the unsaved is "Repent and be born again." Holy life instructions to the believers follow this.

Again speaking to the Hebrew church, Peter said, "For it is impossible for those who were once enlightened, and have tasted of the heavenly gift, and were made partakers of the Holy Ghost, And have tasted the good word of God, and the powers of the world to come, If they shall fall away, to renew them again unto repentance; seeing they crucify to themselves the Son of God afresh, and put him to an open shame" (Hebrews 6:4–6). This truth applies to you and I as well as the Hebrew church. This does not say "some may not," but, some "cannot," repent. Their willingness to repent is no longer possible. This is because they despised the blood that was shed for them. They will not be convicted of sin by the Holy Spirit again after "falling away."

God caused it to be written, "It is impossible" to bring previously enlightened believers who "have tasted of the Holy Spirit" to repentance, should they fall away. He said they cannot be saved. Jesus Christ will not come to be crucified for them a second time. Have you ever heard this text preached and not ignored or twisted and denied? If one cannot come to repentance, they cannot be forgiven of their sins. "Repentance and remission of sins should be preached in His name among all nations, beginning at Jerusalem" (Luke 24:47). This is followed with what God refuses to do, that Christ would have to be crucified a second time to save these people!

Repentance and forgiveness go together. Paul clearly points out that repentance proceeds salvation. "For godly sorrow works repentance to salvation not to be repented of: but the sorrow of the world works death" (2 Corinthians 7:10. Why is it "impossible" for them to come to repentance? Because, as Jesus taught, "No man can come to me, except the Father, which hath sent me, draws him: and I will raise him up at the last day" (John 6:44).

The Holy Spirit, the third person of the Trinity, brings conviction of sin. In their case, He no longer will (John 16:7). This is why Paul taught, "And grieve not the Holy Spirit of God, whereby ye are sealed unto the day of redemption" (Ephesians 4:30).

Backslidings

We all have the potential to slight the Holy Spirit and become a "backsliding" believer. God appeals to the "backsliding" one to repent turn to Him: "Surely as a wife treacherously departeth from her husband, so have ye dealt treacherously with me, O house of Israel, saith the Lord. A voice was heard upon the high places, weeping and supplications of the children of Israel: for they have perverted their way, and they have forgotten the Lord their God. Return, ye backsliding children, and I will heal your backslidings. Behold, we come unto thee; for thou art the Lord our God" (Jeremiah 3:20. We would hope that some heeded this holy appeal. What about the ones who ignored and did not respond?

The Apostle Paul speaks about the end of the road for those who did not and only had one thing to look forward to, God's judgment: "Of how much sorer punishment, suppose ye, shall he be thought worthy, who hath trodden underfoot the Son of God, and hath counted the blood of the covenant, wherewith he was sanctified, an unholy thing, and hath done despite unto the Spirit of grace" (Hebrews 10:29)? When a believer gives in to temptation and continues in sin by their choice, telling their conscience ("spirit man") to be quiet, without genuinely repenting and applying John 1:9, they can come to a place of being "overcome" by sin.

Peter taught:

> "For if after they have escaped the pollution's of the world through the knowledge of the LORD and Savior Jesus Christ, they are again *entangled therein, and overcome,* the latter end is worse with them than the beginning. For it had been better for them not to have known the way of righteousness, than, after they have known it, to turn from the holy commandment delivered unto them. But it is happened unto them according to the true proverb, The dog is turned to his own vomit again; and the sow that was washed to her wallowing in the mire."
>
> 2 Peter 2:20–22

All mankind is tempted including saved people. We must resist and submit ourselves to God. Those who do not resist temptation and enter back into a sinful life are written about as well. Covenants can be broken by man and God acknowledges this fact.

Consider:

Some believe that as long as they attend church services, they will wind up in heaven. Others believe that if you just do good things and don't kill or rape somebody, that you will be accepted. May they find God's answer from His Word to these presumptions, which are based on unscriptural opinions?

Consider what our LORD Jesus Christ tells a church in the book of Revelation. All genuine Bible teachers will agree: these words of admonishment and promises are for all believers and churches. "Thou hast *a few names* even in Sardis which have not defiled their garments; and they shall walk with me in white: for they are worthy" (Revelations 3:4). There were a number of people who attended the Sardis church. A few were considered worthy to walk with our LORD in white. White linen was the righteousness of the saints (Revelations 19:8). Some church attendees should consider the question of "Do I have defiled garments?" This was written for you and I. We can also defile our marriage covenant garments to a point where they are destroyed.

Our Will-based Actions Are Judged

The real basis for God's divorcing of people is that God holds man accountable for his actions. He gave man a free will with a conscience to know right from wrong. Ultimately, God will judge man according to our deeds, actions, and works (Revelations 20:12). The real basis of a God divorcement is not so much what God does. The real basis for God divorcing Israel and His people is God discerning and acknowledging what people do. People break covenants entered into with God. God judges and acknowledges the reality of this breaking.

This same truth applies with the breaking of marriages by people in many divorce situations. The forsaking of the marriage covenant is committed by wrongful, unfaithful actions. They hold an unholy avoidance of dealing with subject matter, which forces a marriage partner to live in pain. They stand in an unholy self-righteousness, not being open to communication to bring healing.

Some hide behind an incorrect doctrinal understanding and will quote that God promises to "never leave or forsake us" (Hebrews 13:5b). This text and the truth it refers to is completely taken out of context when applied to salvation. This text speaks of God's faithful supply and care of the faithful and not to salvation: "Let your conversation be without covetousness; and be content with such things as ye have: for He hath said, I will never leave thee, nor forsake thee. (Hebrews 13:5–6)."

Yes, truly our God is faithful. That is not the problem or question. The problem is, so often man historically is proven to be unfaithful, like an adulterous husband will betray and forsake his covenant with his wife. Likewise, our God simply acknowledges the forsaking of and by His people. He deals accordingly. Otherwise, one is of a mind that people can commit whatever atrocious sin they want after salvation without negative effects. Or the equally foolish thought is that man cannot be tempted or commit sin after salvation.

These foolish people ignore many scriptures, including Hebrews 12;14: "Follow peace with all men and holiness, without which no man shall see the LORD: Also, "Submit yourselves therefore to God. Resist the devil, and he will flee from you" (James 4:7). To resist is solely our responsibility.

We all fail God and sin, regardless of being saved. Jealousy, resentment, un-forgiveness, and pride are sin, just as robbery, murder, and fornication are. We need to continually seek God and His mercy, believing in the atoning blood shed by Jesus our Savior at Calvary, while we grow in faith and sanctification.

Deceived people ignore these truths. Paul admonished us with, "Be not deceived; God is not mocked: for whatsoever a man sows, that shall he also reap" (Gal. 6:7). We always reap the fruit of our decisions, albeit this may take some time. David reaped many years after his wrongdoings.

The forgoing truths are presented so we may see God's judgment in divorcing the unfaithful. Likewise, our God condones the divorce of unfaithful spouses in marriage.

Divorces among Christians and Non-Judgment

In our western world, the unbelieving and unsaved population often seems to get a divorce over trivial matters. Small misunderstandings, miscommunications, and prideful thinking, while being "tired" of a marriage, seem to be enough justification for many divorces. When a divorce takes place between two true believers, there must be a greater justification than these trivial reasons, as the marriage is a covenant made before God Almighty. We must know the genuine God accepted scriptural reasons for a divorce.

When the basis for such a divorce is right, the divorce is due to a just and righteous recognition of the errant partner's actions. Divorce documentation simply memorializes this after the fact.

Many wounded brothers and sisters surround us and are walking in continuous pain. Church leadership bears much of the responsibility for this pain. They are guilty by not declaring the guilt and innocence of those involved, as well as not properly teaching truth regarding this subject.

This lack of a clear, truthful dealing and judgment when appropriate, plus an avoidance of pronouncement to the faith family, causes wrongful critique and opinion. Many innocent believers walk under these clouds bearing silent critique. This is due to church and ministry silence and non-involvement. Where is the shepherd's heart? Where is righteous judgment for the oppressed? Many genuine Christians fade from fellowship and slide back into the world, struggling with wrongful condemnation.

KNOWLEDGE AND GODLY JUDGMENT

Godly Knowledge

Know that the righteous, mature, and godly church will teach believers to bring relationship problems to the church. The righteous and godly church cares enough to teach their adherent's righteous and scriptural people dealings.

There are a few churches that demonstrate leadership ability and heart. This is demonstrated by caring enough to get involved in resolving painful relationship issues. They will have the maturity and heart to address matters in a godly and scriptural manner. We have biblical examples of this heart.

Look at Moses and how he dealt with people problems. He acted out a God-approved righteous leadership example, teaching what people should be doing throughout the Old Testament, as well as today.

"And Jethro, Moses' father in law, took a burnt offering and sacrifices for God: and Aaron came, and all the elders of Israel, to eat bread with Moses' father in law before God. And it came to pass on the morrow, that Moses sat to judge the people: and the people stood by

Moses from the morning unto the evening. And when Moses' father in law saw all that he did to the people, he said, What is this thing that thou doest to the people? Why sittest thou thyself alone, and all the people stand by thee from morning unto even? And Moses said unto his father in law, Because the people come unto me to enquire of God: When they have a matter, they come unto me; and I judge between one and another, and I do make them know the statutes of God, and his laws. And Moses' father in law said unto him, The thing that thou doest is not good. Thou wilt surely wear away, both thou, and this people that is with thee: for this thing is too heavy for thee; thou art not able to perform it thyself alone. Hearken now unto my voice, I will give thee counsel, and God shall be with thee: Be thou for the people to God-ward, that thou mayest bring the causes unto God: And thou shalt teach them ordinances and laws, and shall show them the way wherein they must walk, and the work that they must do. Moreover thou shalt provide out of all the people able men, such as fear God, men of truth, hating covetousness; and place such over them, to be rulers of thousands, and rulers of hundreds, rulers of fifties, and rulers of tens: And let them judge the people at all seasons: and it shall be, that every great matter they shall bring unto thee, but every small matter they shall judge: so shall it be easier for thyself, and they shall bear the burden with thee. If thou shalt do this thing, and God command thee so, then you shall be able to endure, and all this people shall also go to their place in peace."

Ex.18:12–23

Moses, whom God greatly honored, lived out his love for the people and demonstrated his responsibility before God by meeting their needs. Even if this undertaking took all day long. Moses loved and cared for the people. God loved Moses and spoke to him as a friend. We see this was no coincidence. He was willing to sit in judgment from morning to night! Moses was also willing to learn and accepted Jethro's wisdom. He appointed the multiple elders, setting them in place to deal with these needs. He did not "wear away," and the people went to their places "in peace."

Jethro Wisdom

People have not changed and still have their problems. This Jethro counsel is still God's wisdom to us. We need churches which will raise up a mature, plural eldership capable of meeting the believers' needs! Every godly church leader should focus on training and raising up fellow mature elders for a multiple leadership.

Moses was aware of the existing elders in Israel. These elders were an existing group of people whom were acknowledges and invited to join Moses and Jethro at dinner. Moses needed some correction in his self-esteem. He thought he was the only one capable of hearing God's voice to administer justice with wisdom.

Here we run into problems which limit many hurting people, namely few churches taking these scriptures seriously. Few churches teach these Bible-directed truths, and most churches simply ignore them, proven by the fact that they do not teach this to their people. When did you last hear a sermon teaching this truth? Where are the churches where there is a shared authority?

In most churches, the ministry does not have the capability of dealing with such intense problems with patience and depth. These types of problems take a lot of time to hear and handle. Most churches are not structured as directed in the Bible, so are limited.

No Judgment in Churches

Many churches seem to have a one-text theology which is, "Judge not that you be not judged" (Matthew 7:1). Most drunks at the local bar will quote this. They ignore 1 Corinthians 5:12, "Do not ye judge them that are within?" We need to know what we are to judge and what we are not to judge.

The other problem is that most churches will not and do not judge a matter in an authoritative manner. They do not take their godly authority and responsibility seriously. The result is, few churches have a holy and godly scriptural dealing with ungodly and non-submissive adherents. A correct understanding of the proper applicable theology will have to be understood in order to proceed in such dealings. This is due to what Paul stated, "There is no genuine fear of God before their eyes" (Ro. 3:18).

Most churches have a one-man authority pastor structure, with others being advisory and not released to minister to the people. This is similar to Moses's dealing with the elders prior to the Jethro correction. The "take it to the church" problem existed then and is no different today. To adequately handle these problems and, more specifically, to invite believers and welcome them in for problem solving, is godly. Due to the limitation and non-availability of the mostly one-man ministering church elder ministry, this is not a practical reality.

Many are self-esteemed to be the only ones deemed capable of dealing with intense personal ministry. These same leaders do not have a pursuit of raising up fellow leaders.

It is a rare church leadership which will "demand" that a resisting marriage partner attend church dealings. Few will follow through and not back down when tough actions should be taken. A rare few will tell the person who disregards the church's request to attend counseling that if the request is ignored, they will be excommunicated from that church fellowship and are not to attend.

The mature, godly church will do so. They recognize their spiritual authority and responsibility. They act before the seeing eyes of Almighty God (Deuteronomy 10:12)!

Because of the disregard to church authority, their responsibility for the wrongful person ends. An important spiritual truth is that we are not responsible for those who are not submissive to our authority. Conversely, we are responsible for those who accept our authority. We will be held accountable for them in the future judgment by our God: "My brethren, be not many masters, knowing that we shall receive the greater condemnation" (James 3:1).

Few have the godly, intestinal fortitude to publicly announce wrongful people as "out of order." Therefore, few will treat the errant person as a "heathen and publican." Doing this would take genuine holy strength, a stance which is void of "the fear of man which brings a snare (Proverbs 29:25)." It takes an upholding of Bible truth, when one is completely moved by "the fear of the Lord." A church should never be more concerned about or fear the loss of statistics and finances over righteous holy dealings.

The believer must be taught to know their rights and who they are. Bring it to the church and demand a holy, loving, and considerate hearing, complete with a caring follow-up. Continue with the follow-up until problems are discussed and resolved. Demand that the church leadership take a stand in the face of continued wrong.

"If he neglects to hear the church" bears some awful, weighty results. The church leadership who ignores God's directives will also face awful, eternal results. Do not be deceived into thinking that our holy God will turn a blind eye to our dealings. Eternity is a long time when we consider the loss of eternal rewards or eternal life. May we judge matters with the same intent as Paul directed: "That the spirit may be saved in the day of the Lord Jesus" (1 Corinthians 5:5). We must understand that the judgment of erring people is the response of a heart which loves the people, and is meant for good, believing for them to work out their salvation.

Unfortunately, any church judgment is rarely considered as few hear of this non-applied scriptural mandate. A very few Christians are blessed with such a caring leadership, as most are silent. Many are persuaded that loving people is to not get involved with their problems. They simply say, "We love you. We will preach to you, but solve your own problems." Most churches and ministry will not take a stand and in righteousness judge a matter, so there is nothing to "be heard," as the church will not judge nor speak forth a non-existent judgment (1 Corinthians 5:12).

To the Wounded and Struggling Christian

Find a church that will be godly, which applies scriptural mandates. If a church and ministry will not stand with you in righteous dealings, it is the wrong place for you to attend or be in submission to! If the leadership does not stand for a righteous defense of your person and does not care to genuinely deal with your painful problems, they are not shepherds to your soul, but wolves in sheep's clothing.

Some are leeches who want your money and statistics of attendance. Some do not genuinely care for souls and people's personal welfare. Find true shepherds, and avoid "Pharisee" leadership.

Christians, Do Your Part

When we today do not build what is needed for tomorrow, we are heading for a potential disaster. Noah heard from God and spent many years building an ark. He did this to avoid drowning with the rest of the world. The ones that drowned did not know God's voice and mocked Noah for building his ark. The flood did come and most of the people died because they did not prepare for the event.

The safety we create today will preserve us from the storms of life to come. What kind of friendships do we pursue and what kind of church are you attending? Is it a place that is safe and knowledgeable of biblical divorce laws? Is it governed by a leadership who will stand with you in the storms of life? Have you personally studied God's Word? Do you have a sure knowledge and know how to proceed should trials and problems arise within your marriage relationship? Have you surrounded yourself with godly and knowledgeable friends who have a balanced understanding as to biblical love and rights for the believer?

Start building a secure environment now to be prepared for tomorrow, thereby providing protection for you, your marriage, your family, and your eternal destiny.

Do not say, "I am responsible for me and the leadership is responsible to God, and there it ends." Wrong thinking! Our God told the people of Israel who worshipped in the tabernacle, that he held them responsible for the type of leadership they placed over themselves. "And thou shalt say to the rebellious, even to the house of Israel, Thus says the LORD God; O ye house of Israel, let it suffice you of all your abominations… And ye have not kept the charge of mine holy things: but ye have set keepers of my charge in my sanctuary for yourselves" (Ezekiel 44:6, 8). These leaders functioned in ministry but were not allowed to enter into God's presence (read this Bible chapter). Our God holds us responsible for whom we set over ourselves. Few consider this. Our God has not changed.

Heathen Treatment

The application of this Christ-given directive is a mostly non-practiced admonishment and rarely heard of or acted out, even though our Lord Jesus said this is what you do (Matthew 18:17): "And if he shall neglect to hear them, tell it to the church: but if he neglect to hear the church, let him be unto thee as an heathen man and a publican."

When this God-given directive is obeyed according to His Word, we have a huge key in place. The results of such a judgment, if righteously applied, greatly affects the status of a divorced Christian and a potential for a godly remarriage. Here we have a cornerstone fact. This affects our understandings about the issues involved, should the marriage be dissolved and arrive at divorce's door.

Here we are told by our Lord and Savior that a person who is not willing to submit to righteous relationship dealings in a godly fashion is to be treated as a "worldly and unsaved person" (Publican and a heathen). This has a huge effect on the true Christian's standing before God if the marriage falters and disintegrates. This is seen from 1 Corinthians 7:12–15.

Fornication

Fornication is a central factor affecting divorce, and we should weigh this consideration diligently. Fornication, harlotry, and idolatry are a matter of the heart, before any action is evidenced. There is more to adultery than a physical affair with a person outside of the marriage, as many scriptures point out. Spiritual adultery is a heart given to fornication, idolatry, and sin other than a physical sex act. God points this out when expressing the pain of His heart by Jeremiah the prophet: "And it came to pass through the lightness of her whoredom, that she defiled the land, and committed adultery with stones and with stocks (wood)" (Jeremiah 3:9).

People do not have physical sex, committing adultery with stones and wood. They did not perform sex with these green trees but were in idolatry, the worship of nature and other gods, which is "playing the harlot." In the reality of married life, many commit spiritual adultery when we deny our altar covenant vows. This type of adultery is not the righteous basis for a divorce, without a righteous discussion and ultimately with the church involved. This form of an adulterous heart demands confrontation and discussion, as issues such as pornography may bring death to a marriage, when unresolved.

Other examples of this are when the wife does so by denying a husband the headship of the home and marriage after the marriage vows were said to allow God's placement of the husband as the head of the home. Of course, this applies to two believers in the LORD, whom Paul addressed in the marriage vows (Ephesians 5:22). The only way a marriage should exist while having an unbeliever married to a believer is when one of the marriage partners gets saved and the other does not. We are told not to marry unbelievers (1 Co. 7:39).

The husband or wife does so when they focus on "skin" magazines or romantically get hooked on movie actors.

Lusting after others due to visually weighing the possibilities is the wrongful activity spoken of when our LORD Jesus spoke, "But I say unto you, That whosoever looks on a woman to lust after her hath committed adultery with her already in his heart" (Matthew 5:28).

Soaking up pornography and sexually provocative materials is a sin against God and also fits the category of "If your brother (sister) sins against you," as presented in Matthew 18. This provokes grounds for corrective discussions. Playing "the harlot" applies when a marriage partner allows his or her heart to leave the marriage love covenant of "Husbands love your wives and wives honor your husbands." This applies anytime when one places other idols ahead of the marriage commitment (Ephesians 5:21–29).

I know of more than one deceived brother in the LORD, who made hunting, fishing, or golfing a god. There is nothing wrong with going hunting, fishing, or golfing. A good wife will gladly see their faithful, loving husband do some of these activities. However, when these pursuits become a heart-driven fetish paramount to worship while the wife and kids forever take last place, the love covenant is being destroyed. I am acquainted with more than one person who was excessively involved with these pursuits. This same scenario can be attributed to a wife neglecting her family and home, buried in endless soap operas. Some lost their marriage and others have war zone marriages in time, when the believing wife or husband says "no more." Marriage is more than infatuation and sex. We enter into a covenant bond with responsibilities.

When either partner defiles the marriage covenant, we have the right to correct the wrongs. Godly people will not fight this process and will want true love and godliness. Ungodly people will avoid correction with a wrongful anger, or an uncaring or subtle and angry smile.

Ungodly Church Leadership: A Negative Fact

Ungodly leadership will avoid dealing with wrongs, not caring about the pain in their people's lives. They avoid hands-on involvement, while being busy with "ministering to them" by preaching. Ungodly mates will avoid dealing with wrongs, not caring about the pain in their spouse's heart. They will avoid discussions and counseling. This will be exposed when the other partner says, "We need help," and "Let's get others involved," then eventually taking the problem to the church when the situation is not resolved.

Other problems arise when a woman wants to be a "Jezebel," and be of a spirit that demands the headship although never admitting to this as that would not be "spiritual." Then they coerce their husbands into becoming "Ahab" servant-followers. Many women would deny the guilt of fighting for the marriage headship, but cannot deny their obvious fight to be the neck.

Likewise, men can promote what the Bible calls a "Nicolaitan" spirit. Our LORD said He hated this in Revelation 2:15. Nicolaitan means "conquerors of the laity." This describes a control spirit that sucks all genuine life and liberty out of the people by holding them in a mental bondage. Many ministries today are "Nicolaitans." They will demand a controlling headship without caring for the hurting in the congregation, which destroys the reality of a love covenant. True love rejoices in bringing healing to the torn. Genuine love thrills at allowing their spouse to maximize all they can be in life, setting them free, helping each other make choices. Desiring good for each other and having each other's dreams fulfilled is loving and godly.

One divorce I observed was finally formalized after a number of counseling sessions, in which the wife disregarded correction to the truths exposed. The final straw which broke the second marriage for both parties was triggered when she insisted that her teenage son from her first marriage had the right to have his girlfriend sleep in the same room with him, supposedly on the floor. When the believing husband said, "No, this is wrong," she insisted it was her right to approve this for her son. The court documents eventually followed. Unresolved disunity regarding many topics needs to be resolved. If help is needed to achieve this, throw away your pride and humbly accept this.

I remember a preacher whose wife defended her teenage daughter sleeping elsewhere for several nights with friends who the dad did not meet or know. The dad was concerned that boys could be involved. She blocked him from addressing the matter. Her bucking of his rightful place of authority when he wanted to address this matter was one part of the issues in the equation, which led to an eventual divorce. I know there were more. The hard-headed and stubborn demanding of a wrongful headship, and a disregard of rightful authority involving his concerns which needed to be honored and addressed, caused damage. In the same manner, a wrongful, unloving husband focusing on everything else but the marriage is also ungodly.

When personal discussions do not produce resolution with harmony, counseling before believers and elders is a godly pursuit. Should the marriage problems exist in a pastor or elder's home, they should submit to other elders and ministers to address the problems.

In Conclusion

Contrary to some people's theology and beliefs, it is a righteous and godly pursuit to judge matters of sin and wrong between believers. All elders and leadership should know this from God's Word. Apostle Paul specifically stated this with a question to those he addressed, "For what have I to do to judge them also that are without? do not ye judge them that are within?" (1 Corinthians 5:12). Setting wrongs right is a part of leadership responsibility which all should face!

Those who refuse to attend counseling and a holy church involvement upon request by their spouse, although claiming to be Christians, are ungodly. When they will not listen to the church or deny their spouse's request to attend church counseling, they are equal to "heathens," and should be judged accordingly. They have no holy regard for God's Word, the church, and the ministry of God. They place themselves above God's provided authority people. They deny a believer their God-provided rights. This "heathen" status greatly affects one's marital relationship should a divorce ultimately take place. May we be strongly aware of this truth, that whatever we do will be seen and judged by our holy God. As well, whatever we do not do, is seen by His holy eyes.

SCRIPTURAL DIVORCE: SECOND JUSTIFICATION

The Corinthian Church Marriage Questions

Believe it. Church members some two thousand years ago also struggled to deal with marriage problems. As Solomon said, "There is nothing new under the sun." The Corinthian church presented their questions to the apostle Paul. The questions were regarding marriage issues including separation, divorce, and remarriage. The apostle Paul answered these questions under the Holy Spirit and God-inspired anointing, as recorded (1 Cor. 7:1–40).

When studying marriage matters including divorce and remarriage, 1 Corinthians 7 is the key Bible chapter to note. This chapter gives huge answers regarding the second permissible reason for divorce, as well as answers for an acceptable remarriage. The church needs to know and understand what is written in this chapter. This is so vitally important to this topic, so I will include it entirely for the reader's convenience, then deal with the chapter by topic.

Apostle Paul response to the marital questions was:

"Now concerning the things whereof ye wrote unto me: It is good for a man not to touch a woman. Nevertheless, to avoid fornication, let every man have his own wife, and let every woman have her own husband. Let the husband render unto the wife due benevolence: and likewise also the wife unto the husband. The wife hath not power of her own body, but the husband: and likewise also the husband hath not power of his own body, but the wife. Defraud ye not one the other, except it be with consent for a time, that ye may give yourselves to fasting and prayer; and come together again, that Satan tempt you not for your incontinency. But I speak this by permission, and not of commandment. For I would that all men were even as I myself. But every man has his proper gift of God, one after this manner, and another after that. I say therefore to the unmarried and widows, It is good for them if they abide even as I. But if they cannot contain, let them marry: for it is better to marry than to burn. And unto the married I command, yet not I, but the Lord, Let not the wife depart from her husband: But and if she depart, let her remain unmarried, or be reconciled to her husband: and let not the husband put away his wife."

1 Co. 7:1–11

But to the rest speak I, not the Lord: If any brother hath a wife that believeth not, and she be pleased to dwell with him, let him not put her away. And the woman which hath an husband that believeth not, and if he be pleased to dwell with her, let her not leave him. For the unbelieving husband is sanctified by the wife, and the unbelieving wife is sanctified by the husband: else were your children unclean; but now are they holy. But if the unbelieving depart, let him depart. A brother or a sister is not under bondage in such cases: but God hath called us to peace.

1 Co. 7:12–15

For what knowest thou, O wife, whether thou shalt save thy husband? or how knowest thou, O man, whether thou shalt save thy wife? But as God hath distributed to every man, as the Lord hath called every one, so let him walk. And so ordain I in all churches. Is any man called being circumcised? let him not become uncircumcised. Is any called in circumcision? let him not be circumcised. Circumcision is nothing, and uncircumcision is nothing, but the keeping of the commandments of God. Let every man abide in the same calling wherein he was called. Art thou called being a servant? care not for it: but if thou may be made free, use it rather. For he that is called in the Lord, being a servant, is the Lord's freeman: likewise also he that is called, being free, is Christ's servant. Ye are bought with a price; be not ye the servants of men. Brethren, let every man, wherein he is called, therein abide with God."

1 Co. 7:16–24

"Now concerning virgins I have no commandment of the Lord: yet I give my judgment, as one that hath obtained mercy of the Lord to be faithful. I suppose therefore that this is good for the present distress, I say, that it is good for a man so to be. Art thou bound unto a wife? seek not to be loosed. Art thou loosed from a wife? seek not a wife. But and if thou marry, thou hast not sinned; and if a virgin marry, she hath not sinned. Nevertheless such shall have trouble in the flesh: but I spare you."

1 Co. 7:25–28

"But this I say, brethren, the time is short: it remains, that both they that have wives be as though they had none; And they that weep, as though they wept not; and they that rejoice, as though they rejoiced not; and they that buy, as though they possessed not; And they that use this world, as not abusing it: for the fashion of this world passes away. But I would have you without carefulness. He that is unmarried cares for the things that belong to the LORD, how he may please the LORD: But he that is married cares for the things that are of the world, how he may please his wife. There is difference also between a wife and a virgin. The unmarried woman cares for the things of the LORD, that she may be holy both in body and in spirit: but she that is married cares for the things of the world, how she may please her husband. And this I speak for your own profit; not that I may cast a snare upon you, but for that which is comely, and that ye may attend upon the LORD without distraction."

1 Co. 7:29–35

"But if any man think that he behaves himself uncomely toward his virgin, if she pass the flower of her age, and need so require, let him do what he will, he sins not: let them marry. Nevertheless he that stands steadfast in his heart, having no necessity, but hath power over his own will, and hath so decreed in his heart that he will keep his virgin, doeth well. So then he that gives her in marriage doeth well; but he that give her not in marriage doeth better. The wife is bound by the law as long as her husband lives; but if her husband be dead, she is at liberty to be married to whom she will; only in the LORD. But she is happier if she so abide, after my judgment: and I think also that I have the Spirit of God."

1 Co. 7:36–40

These mostly ignored scriptures need to be understood and applied, as they belong to God's Word and are directions for all of us. "All scripture is given by inspiration of God, and is profitable for doctrine, for reproof, for correction, for instruction in righteousness" (2 Tim. 3:16).

To Two Married, True Christians

(1 Corinthians 7:1–11) "Now concerning the things whereof ye wrote unto me:."

The believers of the Corinthian church wrote Paul. They asked him questions about marital matters. The apostle Paul thoroughly answered many questions the church asked him about this subject. Paul first addressed questions regarding rights and difficulties between two married believers. These questions included them asking what their rights were as to separation and remarriage issues.

After this, in verse twelve, Paul follows this with giving directions to a marriage where only one party is a genuine believer, who is married to an unsaved person. This was twice repeated with a believing husband married to an unbelieving wife, or a believing wife married to an unbelieving husband.

The Bible has no instructions about marriage matters to unbelievers. The only message to all unbelievers is to repent from sin and believe on the Savior and be born again, to become part of the believing church. Unsaved, whether religious church attendees or not, are not subject to the spirit of God, "because the carnal mind is enmity against God: for it is not subject to the law of God, neither indeed can be" (Romans 8:7). Going into McDonalds does not make a person into a hamburger, neither does sitting in church services make a person a child of God.

Unless a Christian is truly "born of the Spirit," their minds will be religious or carnal. If religious, they may attempt to live by God's laws and inwardly know they have no peace at the thought of death. The born of the Spirit believer has confronted personal sin "before God," with repentance of the same. This confronting of sin in itself is coupled with a holy vow to turn from anything which is not God pleasing. Simultaneously, one must see Jesus Christ as the holy sin bearer in our stead, placing our faith in His personal love, cross, and shed blood with forgiveness to the believer. This is followed with a life of seeking Him, learning His heart's desire and purposes. Should anyone genuinely take these steps, the result will be an experiential being "born again," and becoming part of the genuine "body of Christ" (1 Corinthians 12:13). Experiencing an initial burst of peace with joy and facing God as "Our Father" will attend this experience.

Be aware that just because a person is "born again" does not mean they now cannot act in a wrongful manner toward God or man. Adam and Eve were without sin when created, yet had the ability to choose in any matters including to sin against God. Being reunited in our spirit man with the spirit of God does not take away our free will responsibilities or make us immune to partaking of sin, especially when we live in a sin- saturated world with temptations.

The scriptures clearly set out the rules of engagement that we as Christians should live by. We are advised as to what kind of God pleasing people we should strive to be. This applies to marriage relationships as well. Paul addressed the believers as to sexual rights and relationship issues. He concluded his discourse with a very specific instruction to them.

Should one separate from their marriage spouse, they should stay single or be reconciled. This "separation time" is a time of sorting out difficulties where a renewed marriage or an eventual divorce may result, hopefully due to righteous reasons, with eldership involvement.

Unequally Yoked Marriage

In 1 Co. 1:12–15, Paul clearly directs Bible truth written to a distinctly different group of people from those he addressed in verses one to eleven. This is doubly set out as explained within verses twelve to thirteen. Paul begins these verses with the statement "To the rest I speak, not the LORD." "To the rest" is a different category of people. These are believers who are living with an unbelieving husband or wife. The difference in how God views this marriage, especially if a divorce should take place, is immense.

Also consider verse forty: "…and I think also that I have the Spirit of God," to balance the statement of "I speak, not the LORD." I believe the intent here is that God is not making a law or rule of conduct, but is allowing for "grace dealings," allowing the believers to decide their limits. We before the LORD know the limits of our capabilities of living with an unbeliever.

The directive of "let her not leave him" is followed with the direction of the truth that we are to attempt to win the unsaved to Christ. However, in this relationship, while prayerfully making efforts to win them to Christ, we do not have to accept continual abuse. God Himself twice affirmed this by "*if they are pleased to dwell*" with you.

Immense Difference

To the two genuinely believing and married people addressed in verses 1–11, God's Word says, "But and if she depart, let her remain unmarried, or be reconciled to her husband."

However, we have a totally different set of instructions for the believer living with the unbeliever. To the "unequally yoked," (a believer living with an unbeliever), God's Word states "But 'if' the unbelieving depart, let him depart. A brother or a sister is not under bondage in such a case: but God hath called us to peace." In God's eyes, a tremendously huge difference exists when a divorce action takes place when the "unequally yoke" are involved. We must understand this matter to properly deal with marriages in a godly manner!

God by His Word states it is all right to allow a divorcement from an unbeliever when our peaceful lives are torn due to the unbeliever not being pleased to dwell with the godly believer.

This "depart" from the "marriage" means the believer is freed from all strings and responsibilities attached to that past marriage, as the "brother or a sister is not under bondage in such cases." God's Word states they are freed. Verses 12–15 are just as relevant as verses 1–11. They clearly depict a different group of people with different separation and divorce rights. These scriptures have largely been ignored! Why?

May all Bible-believing churches, preachers, and believers accept and embrace God's Word regarding this truth. May we honor and uphold the believer who has fought a good fight.

Of course, there are godly terms to living with an unbeliever to be considered, in order to righteously "be freed." However, when one has applied godly principles and this marriage dissolves, the believer is free.

The Key Question Often Missed

What is mostly missed by many churches and preachers is due to the non-application and a sinful disregard of Matthew, chapter 18. The wrong of and disregard of not dealing with marriage debate and grievances in a godly fashion, limits the effect on the believer when dealing with 1 Corinthians, chapter 7 issues. This wrong of non-judgment and the disregard of judging a person who will not flow with godly principles as a "heathen" now limit the transparent and clear dealings of the believer.

The question of whether a believer is living with an unbeliever or a fellow believer is very important. Should a person judged to be as an unbeliever or a heathen by the church in Mathew chapter eighteen, greatly affects the believer's options and position when applying the writings of I Corinthians chapter seven. Face this question with honesty, according to what our LORD Jesus told the church to do, the result is, the wrong-minded person belongs to verse 12–15, a believer living with an unbeliever.

You now have a person our LORD Jesus told us to treat as a heathen living with a believer.

The effect of this truth is huge and needs to be understood by all. Knowing this truth has greater and further consequences, especially when we consider the effect of such a divorce as to which "before God" rules apply at the dissolving of the marriage. Any person so judged by the church now falls within the category of a "heathen" unbeliever living with an unbeliever (Matthew 18:17). It now places them in the same group as unbelievers being separated from a believer, should a divorce take place.

Key Truth

The result of a church dealing is of key and great importance to the divorced person who is divorced from an unequally yoked marriage. Because of the importance involved in this truth and our understanding of these scriptures, let's look at this again.

Our LORD in Matthew, Chapter 18 tells the believer to take brotherly differences to the church for the church to help resolve the matter, working out the conflict of those involved. The church is to impartially set out directives to deal with the issues to bring closure to affect a godly, loving home. This takes real time and is not possible in churches without a mature, knowledgeable, multiple ministry eldership. This should result in a godly, peaceful home when two believers desire God's principles to be applied.

Sometimes we find that one of the marriage partners will refuse to attend church counseling upon request and will avoid such dealings for their personal reasons. Should one of the parties refuse to attend church ministry counseling, they deny their partner their scriptural rights. Should one of the parties be unwilling to work along with this request by their spouse, thereby denying the holy counsel of the church eldership, or not respect the church or spouse's request to attend remedial holy counseling, the church must treat them as an unbeliever (a heathen and a Publican).

The spouse who has a partner who will not attend counseling should simply go to the church and have the leadership request they attend. If they deny the church's request or directive to attend, the church must, as directed by our LORD, treat them as a heathen and a publican. They have disregarded God's Word and despised godly counseling as well. The effect of doing so places them in the position of a believer living with an unbeliever.

In such a case when a believer cannot tolerate the ungodly actions causing pain and destroying their right to peace within the home and marriage, the marriage may come to an end. Should this be the case, the resulting marriage dissolution places them within Paul's instructions as written in verses 12–15. This means that verse fifteen now applies to them. The believer is now "not under bondage" in this case and free. This greatly affects how we are to view the resulting status of the separated and divorced. This freeing includes the right to be remarried if they so choose.

Yes, this scriptural truth does not fit what most churches teach. This is due to a total disregard of the facts stated in these two Bible chapters. Yes, these scriptures and this truth should be studied out and deeply weighed. Then we should face, judge, teach and act out our findings.

No Ball and Chain Marriages

Marriage is the one relationship in holy writ which is comparable to Christ and the church, His bride company. Marriage is a relationship of two people being of one heart, producing a home and life of love, fellowship and joy. Ungodly actions by either party will destroy this picture and reality. When these actions become intolerable and cannot be resolved by the parties involved, God provides instructions to resolve the difficulties. We are not forced to live in an abusive relationship. If we deny these instructions, we deserve the results. We rob ourselves. Any church which does not uphold and encourage our determination to deal with these issues according to biblical directions shares in the ungodly guilt of wrongdoing.

In the USA and other countries, some prisoners have a chain fastened around their ankles with a heavy steel ball attached to the end of the chain. The prisoner can only walk a very short distance with a limited freedom, due to the ball attached to the chain fastened to their ankles. Likewise, a person trapped in an unjust marriage relationship can be limited. All believers need to know two truths.

The first truth is one must have personal Bible knowledge regarding marriage and divorce.

The second truth is they have a biblical recourse to addressing wrong and oppression.

May all godly believers and churches understand that our God never intended that a child of God would be tied to a ball and chain marriage. Living in abusive relationships was never part of His menu. Our God has always intended that the believer has the right to and is instructed to "live in peace." This is why the topic is settled with the words, "but God has called us to peace" (1 Co. 7:15, Jn. 14:27).

Godly Rights of the Believer

The ungodly and unbeliever must allow the believer the right to serve the LORD. The believer must exercise their faith and not hide or be ashamed of their faith. Our faith cannot be denied. Our LORD said that they who are ashamed of Him in this life will experience Him being ashamed of them in future eternity (Mk. 8:38). This scripture says more than the truth of a believer having the right to live in peace. This states that our God tells us that we are called to and expected to live in peace. How can a believer hear His voice in a place and life of strife and turmoil? How can a believer live in kingdom truths, realities, and power when they are oppressed and robbed of peace? Paul explains that "For the kingdom of God is not meat and drink; but righteousness, and peace, and joy in the Holy Ghost" (Rom. 14:17). Those who have entered the kingdom of God have rights. All believers have the right to peace and joy in their lives. We are not to allow an unbelieving and ungodly marriage partner or a judged "heathen," even when they are a self-pronounced Christian, to tear up this peace.

In any case, should a person be judged by the church to be in the same category as the unbeliever and should their lives of co-existing in a marriage with a believer come to a just end, the believer is freed and "not under bondage" (God's Word).

Why has this truth not been upheld in most churches?

- There is a proven ignorance of God's Word and instructions. This is mostly prevalent in the long existing denominations, having roots prior to the nineteenth century. Churches that do not teach about being born again cannot understand this truth, not being capable of discerning a saved person from the religious and unsaved.

- To confirm this, a good example is the Lutheran and Calvinistic churches which have an erroneous view of what they call the "doctrine of predestination." Their interpretation of this doctrine leaves people in limbo, not knowing whether they are saved or not. This teaching is accompanied with if you are saved, you cannot lose your salvation. They commonly teach you will not know for sure if you are saved until you are judged in heaven. How do you now apply these scriptures of a believer living with an unbeliever and make judgments accordingly, when one cannot distinguish the saved from the unsaved?

- More commonly, there is a disregard of God's Word and given instructions to their congregants. Some will say "Are you not being a little hard or judgmental"? No. This can be proven by you, the reader, in short order. When was the last time you heard a preacher present these scriptures and truths portrayed herein? Consider sharing this book with your clergy.

Justifications to Constructive Critique

Critique without answers to a problem is just a critical spirit. Constructive critique has a message as to what should be changed and improved. The following are observations as to what needs to be changed and improved:

1. A church with an unbiblical leadership is not capable of handling the cares of the flock. A caring, genuine shepherd leadership will do all possible to correct and address this need.

2. A disregard for having the church open to in-depth dealings with brotherly differences.

3. Leadership not taking their responsibilities that come with the titles they have taken.

4. A lack of genuine love and concern for the flock and their pain. They just preach platitudes.

5. A leadership who do not know their duties or authority, nor do they regard them seriously.

6. A weak leadership without the intestinal fortitude to take a godly stand in the face of difficult people issues.

7. Many times the real problem is a leadership who think it is more loving and godly to coddle the errant in rebellion than to act per God's Word. Many teach a perversion of love by saying, "Apply grace and just love them with no confrontation." God's Word says, "Treat them as a heathen and a Publican." They hold a Bill Clinton political view demonstrated in ignoring homosexuality in the armed forces ("See not, tell not"). They have a perverted view of God's grace. They avoid confronting the problems.

8. A church that will not judge per 1 Corinthians 6:5, "I speak to your shame. Is it so, that there is not a wise man among you? no, not one that shall be able to judge between his brethren." A weak church compromises truth in not confronting sin.

9. They are not "true shepherds." A church that will not take their God-given responsibility of confronting sin and wrong is not a shelter for anyone struggling with abuse.

Divorce and Rightful Priorities

The LORD of heaven places a greater priority on the peace of His children over a marriage without peace. God's Word states in Proverbs 21:19, "It is better to dwell in the wilderness, than with a contentious and an angry woman." We sometimes make humor with this statement, but this is a holy written fact of wisdom and holy writ truth. "God has called us to peace" (1 Corinthians 7:15) is written after "let the unbeliever depart," and, "a brother or sister is not under bondage in such a case, God has called us to peace." Have you heard this Bible text preached lately? Paul states this in the context of addressing marriage, separation, and divorce!

God says my children are unique and precious to me. I am the great shepherd who leads them into green pastures and beside still waters. The child of God has the God-given right to live a life of peace with joy! The child of God has the divine right and commandment to "love the LORD their God with all of their heart and soul" (Matthew

22:37). This requires the liberty of having a peace of mind with a godly home where there is consideration for the believer. This requires a liberty for the believer to pursue and attend godly functions.

These truths supersede any human marriage covenants when dealing with an unsaved or ungodly marriage partner or those who demonstrate they do not love and honor their spouse and are not "pleased to dwell with them." This particularly applies to those who attempt to deny a child of God the holy right to pursue and live a godly, peaceful life. God places a higher value on the peace and godly walk of His children over an ungodly and less than peaceful, unequally yoked marriage!

If

The "if" word sets boundaries and conditions. "If" *the unbeliever is pleased to dwell* with the believer, then stay together. "Pleased to dwell with" means the unbeliever allows the believer the freedom to peaceably pursue their Christian walk with the LORD. This is not negotiable!

The Word of God never allows a believer to back up from boldly serving Him, and that without shackles. In fact our LORD Jesus said this "commandment:" "And Jesus answered him, The first of all the commandments is, Hear, O Israel; The LORD our God is one LORD: And thou shalt love the LORD thy God with all thy heart, and with all thy soul, and with all thy mind, and with all thy strength: this is the first commandment" (Mk 12:29–30).

The born of the Spirit Christian has entered and sees the kingdom of God and its merits, deserving the kingdom fruit. This kingdom is clearly described: "For the kingdom of God is not meat and drink; but righteousness, and peace, and joy in the Holy Ghost" (Ro. 14:17). How does a child of God have any of these with an unbelieving, abusive marriage relationship? Believers must demand that right. Godly ministry will support them in this demand. Yes, we are to love our neighbor, but loving your neighbor follows the first commandment of love God! The second commandment does not precede the "Love your God" commandment, but follows. Our LORD firmly stated our priority of relationship!

I will never forget how I internally responded to the words a local pastor told a lady I met. She came into a place of ministry which I was in charge of by someone's help. She had a split lip and a black eye from a drunken husband. Upon discussion with her "pastor," she was told to go home, pray for him, and this was part of her cross to bear.

I immediately advised her to move anywhere to a place of safety, offering to help find such a sanctuary from the storm then pray for him from there and not return until this abuse was confronted and dealt with.

Grace and Wisdom
Toward Unbelievers

Godly wisdom does need to be applied, with love and grace, but serving Him is not negotiable.

Jesus clearly taught in Matthew 10:36–38, "And a man's foes shall be they of his own household. He that loves father or mother more than me is not worthy of me: and he that loves son or daughter more than me is not worthy of me. And he who does not take up his cross and follow Me is not worthy of Me."

Some will say this does not specifically address a husband or wife, even though it clearly addresses those "of his household." May we not forget Christ's teaching: "And every one that has forsaken houses, or brethren, or sisters, or father, or mother, *or wife,* or children, or lands, for my name's sake, shall receive a hundredfold, and shall inherit everlasting life. (Matthew 19:29).

This is not a simple matter. However, these central truths are factual and scriptural, although mostly denied in reality, if not in stated unbelief.

However, a godly person will make sacrificial and great effort to love and win their spouse to Christ.

Give Instructions to the "Unequally Yoked"

Paul admonishes the unequally yoked believer to do their godly all to be a loving and Christ-reflecting mate. This is also found in 1 Peter 3:1–2: "Likewise, ye wives, be in subjection to your own husbands; that, if any obey not the word, they also may without the word be won by the conversation of the wives; While they behold your chaste conversation coupled with *fear*" (respectful reverence). The intent is to be a witness and win the unbeliever to Christ.

This is a godly truth preached from most believing evangelical church pulpits. I greatly agree.

However, this is rarely balanced with the other truths expressed in the same Bible (Matthew 18:17, 1 Corinthians 7:15). Christians need to know their rights and liberty to pursue a godly Christ-worshipping life with peace.

A Christian is not a doormat to be stomped on. God Himself had it written that if the unbeliever is not pleased or does not want to tolerate your godly life pursuit, let them depart! Furthermore, "A brother or a sister is not under bondage in such cases." This means freedom. Free from the marriage. Free from guilt condemnation. Free to continue with a God-fearing life pursuit.

The genuine painful struggle one will face is the question of: *Did I do my righteous all to show love and grace, while taking a stand for my God provided rights?* One must have a clear conscience before God in all matters, or one will not have a resulting peace, regardless of a marriage separation, divorce or remarriage. This peace can only be obtained by a sure knowledge of God's Word as to what is truth and right, along with the sure knowledge we have done our all to apply His Word.

RIGHTEOUS LOVE AND JUDGMENT

Wrong Examples of Judgment

My heart aches for a wonderful church secretary whom I was acquainted with. She is not serving God the way she used to, and frankly has "backslid." I do not justify her, yet I understand how she got there. Some should "shake in their boots" with fear if they faced the fact that they have offended one of God's little ones and caused this little one to stumble (Matthew 18:6).

She was serving God and woke up one morning to find her hubby gone with another female. The church leadership never publicly declared her guilt or innocence in this matter. They only removed her from her faithful place of service to God, because of "what the people and the world might think."

Imagine the holy anger of the LORD due to this travesty of injustice. This lady had been crucified and abandoned by her husband, then critiqued and adversely dealt with by the church. This course of action was supposedly taken over godly and, in fact, ungodly appearances. There was no publicly pronounced judgment announced in this situation, which was a grave injustice. This damaged saint was thrown under a gray blanket cloud. I also did not hear of any plans to lovingly make restitution to the secretary.

I am aware that in the Deuteronomy and Ruth examples *all the people knew and approved the verdict.* This case took place in a church where none heard the truth and no verdict was declared. This took place in a "full gospel church," demonstrating unworthiness for such a description.

Case in Point

I received a long distance call from a young Christian lady struggling with how she should advise her friend who lived near my town. The friend was facing a probable divorce. My caller is a friend of a "Christian couple." The wife became a born-again Christian during her teenage years, and her husband was raised in a genuine Christian home. She explained this story and related these factors.

Apparently, the shaky marriage had a number of problems. The "Christian" husband told his wife, "If you do not provide the sex I require when I want it, I will go elsewhere to get my needs met and you will be at fault." To add to the struggles, her husband had recently admitted to being involved with the child molestation of his younger sister. His actions included him saying, "Get out," along with, "If you leave our two children with me, I will tell the appropriate government office that you have abandoned them. If you take them and run, I will call the police and tell them you have abducted them." My immediate response was to tell the caller to advise the young Christian women to include her church authorities, but first of all, go to the godly church-attending father-in-law. The response was that the "godly father-in-law" had shown great bias toward the son, and favored the son's negative stories. She had lost confidence in approaching him. As for the church, she had already done so.

The church had sent a genuine man of God (whom I respect), a minister within their church, to counsel with the two of them. According to the potential divorcee, the counseling went fine until the husband was addressed in areas of ungodly behavior which he did not want to discuss. He refused to attend any more sessions. Ultimately, they got divorced. I personally observed him spending social time with other females in a public place prior to the divorce.

The immediate tearing of many hearts took place. The divorcee resulted in being a single mother with children, eventually living in a common-law relationship. The believers in that church never heard a pulpit verdict in the matter. This left them with their gray blanket opinions. Those involved will justify one or the other. Polarization of friends and family resulted. Within the family of God, confusion reigned and gossip flew. Every church with no godly judgment is widespread with gossip. People problems always exist and, when unresolved, foment barriers to true fellowship.

The Christian woman who had regularly attended church with a godly pursuit is no longer attending any church and has gone into the world. Her former husband got remarried and is satisfied with his position as evidently the church is too. He partakes of communion, and he belongs to a socially acceptable church family. He is an "upstanding" church member. *The church leadership failed both of them!*

The Real Answer Should
Lie in the Church

The ministry whom I respect should never have dropped the ball. He knew of the pain and heartaches of the young couple involved. In his eldership's arena of taking heed over the flock, he should have stayed with this situation until it was resolved. If he felt inadequate, he should have involved other elders. He should never have allowed the young man to control the choice of coming in for counseling, as long as the elders were not satisfied with the conclusion of the matter.

Perhaps the Christian father and mother-in-law should have sat in on an open conversation to dispel infighting and expose truth. The church leadership should have forced the young man to attend a church hearing and counseling involvement, advising him of an ultimate negative judgment to be decreed should he disregard this attendance.

A godly dealing at this level, due to facing *the issues* involved and then enforcing forgiveness teachings when and if the issues are addressed, is imperative. Facing the issues in an honest, firm, and gentle manner, should bring an eventual godly end to the matter. Prayerfully and hopefully, the matter would be resolved in a positive vein. The Apostle Paul explaining love said that hope believes all things. We hold onto hope until it is proven to be baseless in reality.

If one of the parties will not listen to and disregards holy and wise church input, the church should rebuke them publicly. "Them that sin rebuke before all, that others also may fear" (1 Timothy 5:20). This public awareness of the matter is a double-edged sword. It allows the believing body to know the truth according to an appointed leadership and dispels gossip and gray clouds. Secondly, this may be a deterrent to the person considering an unrighteous disregard and a dishonoring of godly leadership.

Plead with them to be godly. In some cases when gross sin is involved, bind the guilty unrepentant person over to Satan "for the destruction of the flesh." This is rarely considered, although it is God's directive (1 Corinthians 5:5). We must correct the wrong, bring unity, and defend the innocent. It is sad that some reading this will disregard these statements, since they choose to disregard these scriptures as well. Yet they will name Christ as LORD of their lives.

Church Responsibilities, Especially in Divorce Matters

- Provide Godly Biblical teachings and direction.
- Determine right from wrong. Clear and uphold the innocent.

- Identify the guilty and direct them to genuine repentance.

- Restore the penitent, always striving for unity and restoration.

- Teach all to lead a holy life with true peace. This is our responsibility as elders over the flock.

We need a multiple godly, mature eldership to fulfill this responsibility.

Job, Whom God Bragged On

Job was a unique believer who ultimately was hugely blessed after some trials. Job was the saint God bragged about at a special heaven-called meeting. He had a walk of "chosen fasting." He spent time dealing with the pain and suffering of others.

> "Because I delivered the poor that cried, and the fatherless, and him that had none to help him. The blessing of him that was ready to perish came upon me: and I caused the widow's heart to sing for joy. I put on righteousness, and it clothed me: my judgment was as a robe and a diadem. I was eyes to the blind, and feet was I to the lame. I was a father to the poor: and the cause which I knew not, I searched out. And I break the jaws of the wicked, and plucked the spoil out of his teeth."
>
> Job 29:12–16

Job lived out the fast our mighty God respects and approves of. May we equally receive the LORD's blessing as we minister to others in their hour of need: "Is not this the fast that I have chosen? to loose the bands of wickedness, to undo the heavy burdens, and to let the oppressed go free, and that ye break every yoke...Then shall thy light break forth as the morning, and your health shall spring forth speedily: and thy righteousness shall go before thee; the glory of the LORD shall be thy reward" (Isaiah 58:6). May we love others enough to live this kind of walk and receive our God's reward.

How our God rejoices when He sees His saints ministering to the needs of the wounded and defenseless! When we apply godly church judgment, we will be as Job, whom God bragged on in heaven's meeting. Now apply this to marriage wrongs affecting many around us!

Divorce and Gray Blankets, Guilt

Much has been written on the topic of divorce, including many books about divorce recovery. Mostly, they focus on inner emotional healing. I am an advocate for divorce recovery but am more concerned about the believer's eternal soul and God relationship, with peace before God. This goal should include forgiveness of sins in failure.

One of the major areas of trauma resulting from divorce is guilt. Guilt can be the result of Holy Spirit conviction which is good, or a wrongful condemnation due to how we perceive either God or man to view our actions. Knowing truth and righteousness to guide our actions dispels guilt.

If we correctly understand theology on this subject, we will be capable of ministering to the divorced in guilt matters, rather than loading them up with wrongful guilt.

How can we minister to those involved when we cover all with a gray blanket? We will have gray unless black-and-white issues of truth are established. Many walk away from God, not being able to live with their present circumstances and also not being capable of lifting their heads up toward the heavens. A good Bible knowledge of what one should do and may do lifts shrouds of darkness. Truth brings light to direct us in our paths.

To seek out understanding of scriptural standards about this topic is godly and essential. This means that we need to search out theology. Knowledgeable study will enable us to minister correctly to this painful arena of human failure. Many wounded brothers and sisters surround us, walking in continuous pain. Much of this is due to the apathy and the guilt of weak church leadership, and is multiplied due to a wrong church leadership structure.

Summary

To sum this up, there are factors which contribute to the wrong imposed on the righteously divorced. Besides spousal abuse, the actions and inactions of fellow believers and especially the church leadership greatly enhance the pain and trauma. When gutless leadership does not take responsibility applying a holy and godly standard, pain and death within the flock results.

Often churches leave the people travelling through life's desert with no Moses to bring righteous judgment. A wrong and lacking leadership structure, combined with no godly standards being set, make for a great lack in the church. This especially applies when dealing with the divorced. Most people hold "gray blanket" views toward the divorced, believing both parties are somewhat guilty. Without holy standards this is normal in most churches, as guilt or innocence is rarely pronounced. This is never the case in God's sight and should not be in man's sight.

Due to this lack of ministry governance, on many occasions the innocent saints are greatly wronged. Often, due to a lack of church judgment, the innocent are declared guilty by the people, while the church is guilty of not declaring innocence or guilt.

Some defer from a godly pronouncement, fearing man and a lawsuit. God demands we defend and uphold the righteous. Consider a simple statement such as "There are proven unresolved difference s between Mr. and Mrs. Smith. We honor Mrs. Smith and her values in the difficult recent divorce. Mr. Smith has not followed godly instructions and values this church upholds."

Ministry and Church Guilt

Should wrongful inactions be involved when marriage difficulties exist, these inactions will contribute to a divorce which could have been alleviated. Often the blame may be shared between wrong leadership and the divorced. Often church leadership will share in the guilt, because they contribute by their lacking inaction. The guilt is due to their non-involvement and not making black-and-white out of gray situations. Leadership must maintain and insist upon righteous dealings among believers, establishing a holy church. Their guilt is due to "non-government."

We see so much "non-government" when there is a visible but non-functional leadership. Much of this is due to ministry lacking a true shepherd's heart. They will not intervene with a mandatory holy love counseling to prevent the divorce. Yet they will criticize after the fact by limiting the divorced. May the LORD have mercy upon all involved. With eldership involvement, many divorces could be avoided.

Many of your fellow believers are divorced. If these divorces took place while they attended your church, the church leadership had responsibility towards the believers involved. If guilt was not assessed and disclosure not made to the congregation, they failed those involved whether by ignorance or intent. The result will be that the congregation and all who know them will now make their own limited assessments, victimizing the godly and innocent.

Paul wrote to the leadership, "Them that sin rebuke before all, that others also may fear" (1 Timothy 5:20). Ministries who fear God more than man will obey this. Out of a concern for their flock and concern for the couple involved, they will act. The real test is, "Did the leadership clearly set out godly standards for those involved, and did they press for righteous involvement, exercising their authority and responsibility?"

We Judge in God's Sight

Many say, "Let the LORD judge them and how can we know the truth"? God says, church leadership, you hear them out and determine the truth and discern by my Spirit. Govern and deal with my people, with holy and righteous judgment. (1 Corinthians 5:12) Dealing with and declaring righteous judgment is a tough field of the reality of life. Consider how often Moses faced this reality as he led God's people across the wilderness, including the Korah dealing (Numbers 16:24).

Publican and Heathen Treatment

If you have never experienced a person publicly identified as a publican and a heathen, then this writing is proven as needful. The absence of seeing anybody judged as a heathen or an unbeliever with unrepented of wrong shows the need for biblical teaching regarding this topic, which greatly affects divorce statistics.

It is our duty in the "nitty-gritty" of church life to follow scriptural observations. The proven absence to apply church judgment in accordance to biblical obedience is obvious. This absence attests to the need for drawing attention to the mandates given by Jesus himself. If this is not the norm, it is because ministry leadership has not properly taught these truths. Or they have disregarded the scriptures written regarding this topic. Mental and unholy scissors, deleting passages of holy writ by discarding the truths presented, are common. We must not disregard Christ-given instructions.

Always attempt to achieve restoration with true peace in marital discord. However, if this cannot be achieved due to someone refusing to attend or deal with godly church input, or to genuinely face discerned issues during counseling, deal with them. When they, upon hearing holy correction, refuse to heed the church-discerned course of correction and judgment with a disregard for authority, treat them "as a publican and heathen." Pronounce judgment and allow the believer a righteous divorce from ungodly spouses who disregard God's Word and principles, being the cause of a home without peace.

Many want appearance and the visual status as King Saul desired above truth. Samuel spoke to Saul in correcting his wrong heartedness in focusing on appearances while informing him of the loss regarding his standing as King over Israel, per the Word of the LORD. Saul was more interested in Samuel honoring him visibly by pressing Samuel to honor him before the elders and the people by attending a visibility function (1 Samuel 15:22–30).

We must honor God's Word by righteously judging and releasing believers. Give the innocent hope for a future, godly marriage. Deal with the stubborn and those guilty of resisting godly correction and counsel.

If they move to another church, simply pray for them and do not be anxious about their behavior. Send the judgment of God with them, and trust God. If we will act, God will act. We are not sentencing them to hell. That's God's arena of judgment, as He knows the end of the matter.

We are desirous of seeing them repent and turn to avoid a future hell and a lost eternity. Advise them on the way out of the door that they are to follow Philippians 2:12, "Wherefore, my beloved, as ye have always obeyed, not as in my presence only, but now much more in my absence, "work out your own salvation with fear and trembling."

The church they flee to giving them sanctity, without dealing with their situation and yet allowing them peaceful refuge, will reap from the LORD. That is His department. When new people come to us, we should communicate and get some knowledge of their history. We want to face issues without looking for cash flow and attendance numbers. God will ultimately deal with all of us according to our works. A proper functioning eldership will gently seek out the background of the new arrival, then help them clean up any areas which need to be addressed.

Declared Heathens (Unbelievers)

When a person denies another believer the benefit of attending a genuine church complaint hearing and does not listen to righteous and holy church guidance for godly correction, they are to be considered as a publican and a heathen. This clearly places them in the same category as an unbeliever, as spoken of in Matthew chapter 18.

In verses 12 and 13 of in 1 Corinthians chapter 7, we read the word "if." This conditional word is holy God inspired. May we measure the usage of this word accordingly.

If! If the unbeliever is pleased to dwell with the believer, let them not leave the unbeliever. Let us face this head on. Verse 15 says if the unbeliever is not pleased to dwell with a believer, and there is an ultimate separation of ways (verse 15), "a brother or a sister is not under bondage in such cases: but God hath called us to peace." When one is "not under bondage," they are set free to marry, should they so choose.

I recall the heartache and problems my oldest daughter faced. She married a supposed believer, which may have been the case. This person turned to drugs and other sinful actions. The last straw was when he charged into their home which he had not attended for a few days, unplugged the TV the kids were watching, and left with it. Besides other abusive areas of their marriage, the end finally resulted in a divorce. Who before a holy God would deny this young mother the right to get married to a godly man, who would be a dad to her two kids? She did and has enjoyed a godly marriage since.

May we have the intestinal fortitude to declare them "not under bondage." May we have the bowels of mercy to judge the matter. As an authoritative ministry, declare a verdict of innocence when appropriate (Philippians 2:1). God requires this: "Where no counsel is, the people fall: but in the multitude of counselors there is safety" (Proverbs 11:14).

We must correct problems, defend the innocent, and declare guilt. Of course it is impossible to know guilt or innocence unless the leadership gets intimately involved and spends real time to really know the circumstances. This is not feasible without a multiple eldership.

The believer, who is "not under bondage," is *free,* and should be judged and upheld as such by the leadership! Free to marry or not marry. The only limits imposed on those who are "loosed" from such a situation" are found in 1 Corinthians 7:27–28. These are the same that apply to any child of God. Should they choose to marry, they are to marry "in the LORD" (1 Corinthians 7:39).

Some get all hung up on verse 15, "if the unbeliever depart." Yes, the believer should stay in the marriage if at all possible and attempt to win the unbeliever to Christ, as the believer is a sanctifying (cleansing) agent in the marriage. However, they are not to be trapped in the marriage as a caged animal. They should not feel as though they are imprisoned with hopelessness when a wrongful partner will not discuss and address issues causing struggle and pain.

Wrong Marriage Basis and Union

The unbeliever or self-pronounced "Christian" may not want to depart and may want to "physically" stay. The benefit package may have sexual, financial, and maid or Mr. Fix-It qualities, and not necessarily in this order. May we assess the situation involved with holy integrity, and counsel accordingly, praying for God's mercy and wisdom.

Compared to true love, our God Himself defined adultery as something more than a physical sex act outside of a covenant relationship (Matthew 5:28). Adultery is also a matter of the heart. When an unbeliever insists on an open display of disrespect for the values of the believer, causing the believer pain and a loss of living in peace, this should be addressed.

Should the unbeliever show a loveless disdain and be insensitive for the habits and lifestyle of the Christian by not allowing them to act out their Christian lifestyle, they are opening a door for the believer to leave the marriage. This means the unbeliever must be loving and sensitive and not be abusive with issues such as open pornography, abusive acts or language, drunkenness, or ridiculing the believer's faith and devotional habits. Likewise, the Christian must also be equally sensitive and not demand Christian devotions from the unbelievers.

Many problems exist. A so-called "brother" turned his wife cold, due to insisting it was his right to indulge in pornography, causing her to be incapable of response in private family relationships while being unwilling to attend counseling. At the divorce, was she at fault? Another "sister" determined sexual involvements were for procreation and otherwise not needed. Counseling with the elders may have resolved this misunderstanding. The avoidance of love and intimacy due to the complaint of a three hundred sixty-five days a year headache, should be discussed. Work at avoiding a divorce.

May we apply true, godly, sensitive, and gracious judgment in the church of Jesus Christ. May we love God and the family of God enough to apply commanded holy biblical truths. May we attempt to be discreet, considering that love hides a matter whenever we can, applying Christian grace. May we help people in pain and headed for wrong by judging and declaring truth.

Love covers a multitude of sins. It is all right to defend our person by being gracious yet honest with others and ourselves. May our love for others, and especially the saints, be strong enough to determine truth, when dealing with any matter, including marriage struggles. May we have the godly intestinal fortitude to block the impenitent from fellowship and declare sin for what it is.

May we always have our focus toward forgiveness and a total restoration of the penitent, while being a wall of preservation to God's children and saints.

It will take the "multitude of counsel" from a scriptural multiple ministry eldership to do this. Praise God! By His leading and grace, this is possible. Help us, dear LORD, to address this great need.

PROBLEMS IN OBTAINING A RIGHTEOUS DIVORCE

Spouse and Church, Wrongful Response

The first problem is a spouse who refuses to allow marriage difficulties to be counseled by genuine church leadership. They who refuse to attend church counseling, upon request of their hurting spouse, are instantly guilty of a following divorce. Yes, both parties may be guilty of wrong. However, should one of them refuse to attend church involvement, regardless of perceived wrongs perpetrated by the one who requests attendance to church counseling, they are to be considered as an unbeliever due to having a disregard for church eldership.

They have robbed their partner from dealings in the court of grace and holiness. They have shown an intolerable disrespect for God-provided authority and instructions, and as such are ungodly. They have denied their spouse the right to have problems dealt with via the involvement of God-provided ambassadors.

However, the second problem for many believers is the absence of or availability of a mature godly "stand up" church leadership. Many are unwilling to deal with member marriage problems due to immature and wrong-minded leadership limitations. Nevertheless, request and insist that they attend to the matter. Persuade them by biblical textual truth to be involved and discuss issues.

Many offer a sympathetic ear or pray Pharisee prayers over the wounded but will not engage in genuinely dealing with problems or a "staying the course" until a holy resolution is achieved. Many will simply say, "Oh well, what can we do?" if the "other" spouse does not want to attend. The church eldership are guilty of wrong and are to be disregarded should they not bow to the word of God, the Bible, and its truths presented therein. They must accept their responsibility.

The church leadership who does not intervene, knowing that someone within the marriage desires church counseling, or when the second party refuses to make themselves available, shares in the guilt with the non-attending, unwilling person. They do so by not carrying out their godly duties. Worse yet, many church leaders send their wounded adherents to secular counselors. God have mercy on them.

Refusal to Attend

To those who refuse to attend, it is a sin to hold silence with an unwillingness to allow godly help to assist and intervene. We do not have the right to withhold ourselves from honest, open, and caring conversation. The loveless and stubborn action of not being willing to present oneself before church ministry eldership, can be the root cause of the "putting away" Paul refers to in 1 Corinthians chapter seven. This prideful denial of a believer's Christ-given right is loveless, proven by an unwillingness to address painful struggles in a spouse's heart and mind.

My experience has taught me that those refusing to attend counseling are usually bitter and self-righteous, usually mixed with pride. They usually want to hide issues which they do not want to address, while determining to look good to others. They will vent bitterness and act in subtleties and untruth. The statement, "We do not need any help and can fix this ourselves," when a spouse requests help is wrong. Meanwhile, anger and other destructive abusive behavior is common. Their pride will not allow them to discuss personal problems with leadership or others. Their love of self and their image consciousness is larger than the pain and struggle within their spouse's heart. This god of image is their real god, and this god looms larger than the love for their hurting spouse.

Sometimes it is an unwillingness to forgive their bitterly held stance against their spouse, subtly scheming a way out with the intent of maintaining honor in the sight of those around them. We all make choices. In a divorce action, the real divorce took place long before the papers were signed. Whoever filed for the divorce, and initiated the paper work, may simply be the one who mopped up the floor after the milk was spilled.

The real issues are to be sorted out by those involved with the help of others when needed. When they are unable to do so, they must deal with this through the church. Anyone who is unwilling to do so is ungodly. Those who will not attend or listen to godly church counsel must be treated as a heathen and publican.

My apostle friend, Ernesto Balili, from the Philippines raised the question, "What if the spouse attends a different church holding different standards?" The answer is to show the offending spouse the scriptures that are applicable, as well as the leadership of the "other" church. If the spouse does not bow before God's Word and will not heed the path which may produce peace, make up your own mind if you want to stay in the marriage. The "other" church leadership will be partakers of God's judgment in time, should they ignore His Word. Usually, God gives all "Jezebels" time to repent. He always acts and does not forgive those unrepentant of sins (Luke 17:3, Revelation 2:20).

Judgmental?

Some will no doubt ask, "Now, brother, are you not getting a little bit judgmental, or legalistic?" No! Being judgmental is a constant attitude to be avoided. However: Yes! I do judge some matters, and should all of us not do so? When we do not demonstrate to our people what the holy judgment in a dispute is, we rob the innocent. We also rob the guilty due to not raising a godly standard, acting as a defense to their person and souls. In 1 Timothy 5:20, Paul taught his ministry protégé, "Them that sin rebuke before all, that others also may fear." Those who may be tempted to be ungodly will find this to be a deterrent to sinful actions. Those who are innocent will be upheld with holy righteousness.

Why is this rarely applied when this is a clearly written Bible truth? Mostly because we do not tremble at God's Word. We take what we want and what is convenient without causing "waves."

This holy judgment, dealing with painful sin and wrong, will stop gossip and avoid separation within the body. This allows those with opinions to come and testify before a judgment is rendered, and silences them after the verdict. May we *love* our people enough to get involved. Declare a holy and righteous standard in the real issues of life, including marital problems.

Common Historic Problems

I know of a ministry whose wife refused to attend church counseling, but made appearances to others that she was willing. When rightful counseling was requested to bring peace, and the scripture of "God has called us to peace" was quoted, they simply said, "I do not believe that." This prideful blindness leads to avoidance of problem solving and denies the statements of Our LORD, "Take two or three others, and then to the church." The divorce that followed was certainly affected by this position being taken.

Greater problems are due to a church and ministries not being approachable. Many of them avoid genuine involvement. *Share this book with them.* Challenge them to study the textual theology set forth herein. Better yet, get a copy of *Fivefold Ministry Churches* and share this with your eldership.

Wrong Theology

Most of the old-time, denominational churches do not allow for divorce. Many place a totally negative slant on righteously divorced believers. This is due to bad doctrine and lacking knowledge.

For example, in the Philippines, where the majority of people are Roman Catholic, a person can only pursue an "annulment" of the marriage. In reality, this is only available to the wealthy. A reliable source, a Spirit-filled born again Catholic sister in the LORD, has struggled to deal with an unfaithful husband who maintains adulterous side interests. The cost for her to pursue an annulment at this time is approximately three years' wages. The church controls an "annulment process." These struggling un-divorced people cannot remarry, being held in limbo. The result is that many will be remarried by a mayor or judge, avoiding a church marriage. Often due to their poverty situation, they will simply move in and live common-law.

Since the only way to get a divorce (annulment) over there is through the Catholic-dominated government, her options are limited. Besides that, what are the logistics of an annulment anyway? She has been married for thirteen years at this writing and she has two children by him.

How perverted can a church hierarchy be, to "annul" that which they previously bound before God? Besides that, they will exonerate the adulterous husband, who will go to confession and be told to pray the rosary or say ten Hail Marys and/or give money?

Why does a financial payment to the church answer a moral issue before a holy God? Besides, the godly and betrayed woman is left with the ungodly dilemma Jesus spoke of. She may be "caused to commit adultery." She is exiled to a lonely life as a married, yet single, leper. And that is due to her husband's infidelity. What an atrocious and unrighteous dealing with God's people! What a sinful crime against God and man. In time, everyone's judgment is due; may they consider that.

God's Righteous Judgment

Our just and Holy God will not leave a righteous believer bound to such an unjust bondage. He says divorce is a holy and righteous option for you when you are a child of God. This is almost the worst, but not the only, example of unjust and unholy church wrongdoing. Meanwhile, the poor Catholic believers are bound by mental prison bars. They believe what they are told, that Peter's lineage holds the keys to heaven, so do not buck them. Someday the believing community will rise up and change this form of horrible bondage in their government.

Similar problems exist in the largest "Full Gospel," or Pentecostal denomination, which is closer to my personal beliefs since they uphold a separate experiential "baptism in the Holy Ghost" doctrine. When someone in the ministry gets divorced, they are now marked "rejected from ministry." This seems to be regardless of the circumstances involved. Some of their preachers from their pulpits proclaim to the entire congregation that any person who is divorced "no matter why," cannot remarry, nor can they hold a place in productive ministerial and eldership involvement. These are mostly and often judged without a trial.

It seems they never or rarely declare from the pulpit the innocence of an honorably divorced victim. They thereby bind the result of sin committed by a wrongful spouse upon the righteous. Responsible, godly, and holy people are now critiqued by their fellow unknowing members. They do not sit in judgment with the multitude of counsel to determine the facts, yet give a blanket judgment by their pulpits of silence.

My wife, Siony, was a victim of this atrocity of injustice, being divorced from an adulterous husband prior to marrying me. However, after such a morning sermon, she cried out to God about the injustice. Immediately upon opening her Bible, she read where it opened, in 1 Corinthians chapter seven, the LORD setting her free. This transpired well before meeting me at an inter-denominational mission's conference where I was the speaker.

God's Mercy Intervention

The answers to all of these circumstances lie within the Bible, God's Holy Word.

The prophet Isaiah wrote in Isaiah 61:1–3:

" The Spirit of the LORD God is upon me; because the LORD hath anointed me to preach good tidings unto the meek; he hath sent me to bind up the brokenhearted, to proclaim liberty to the captives, and the opening of the prison to them that are bound; To proclaim the acceptable year of the LORD, and the day of vengeance of our God; to comfort all that mourn; To appoint unto them that mourn in Zion, to give unto them beauty for ashes, the oil of joy for mourning, the garment of praise for the spirit of heaviness; that they might be called trees of righteousness, the planting of the LORD, that he might be glorified. "

When "Pharisee" religious leaders do not understand and apply these truths, get away from them! The apostle Paul wrote in 1 Corinthians 11:1, "Be ye followers of me, even as I also am of Christ." This infers Paul saying, do not follow me if I am not following Christ.

Christ's followers teach and uphold the entire word of God, with love for His people. They respond to Christ's directive to Peter: "If you love me, feed my sheep" (John 21:17). Do not simply take their money while wearing clerical robes, demanding high seats and accepting the "Reverend" title.

Unequally Yoked with Unbelievers

We must see the difference of instructions provided to the unequally yoked believer, in 1 Corinthians 7:12–15, from what is written in verses 1–11, to two believers. When we do not understand this, and most do not, we are incapable of properly dealing with the church divorce issue!

This is clear from verse twelve, where we read: "But to the rest speak I, not the LORD: If any brother hath a wife that believeth not, and she be pleased to dwell with him, let him not put her away. And the woman which hath an husband that believeth not, and if he be pleased to dwell with her, let her not leave him."

To the Rest...

In this statement, "to the rest speak I," describes instructions to a distinctly different group of people, being the "unequally yoked" married people. "To the rest" is described as a believer living with an unbeliever. We need to judge all matters with these scriptural distinctions in mind. Two believers in Christ should never be judged with the same standards as the unequally yoked, separately identified, and written about.

The rules for the married in Christ are to avoid divorce and stay separated and single or be reconciled (1 Corinthians 1:10). Should a separation between two believers take place, they are not to remarry but work out their differences, while appealing to the church for help. If one of them disallows church involvement, the believer is now living with an ungodly, esteemed unbeliever.

A very different set of rules apply "to the rest." When the unbeliever is "not pleased" to live with the believer should the marriage dissolve, the believer is "not under bondage," and may remarry.

Seven Problems Identified

There are a number of problems at this time, as to a person being perceived as holy and correct by the family of God, in the sight of God where divorce is concerned.

Some of the problems that need to be overcome are:

1. Poor and limiting theology by many churches.

2. Wrong doctrinal understanding by most believers as to Biblical divorce.

3. Churches with a limited and wrong (unscriptural) ministry structure.

4. Believers not welcomed or encouraged to attend a church court hearing of problems.

5. Church leadership deferring or refraining from judging sin and wrong.

6. Churches not speaking forth guilt and innocence from the pulpit in divorce matters.

7. Church leadership deferring from declaring publicly that a person is to be treated as an unbeliever, and a heathen. This "wimp" stance, leaves the righteous believer under a tainted cloud, sharing in the none judged guilt.

Point One in Summary

The Bible is God's Holy Word, and 2 Timothy 3:16 declares, "All scripture is given by inspiration of God, and is profitable for doctrine, for reproof, for correction, for instruction in righteousness." This includes the right to a holy divorce for the innocent party of an adulterous marriage partner (Matthew 5:32 and Matthew 19:9).

We must distinguish between an unbeliever living with a believer and two believers united in marriage. Of course, to discern this distinction will be very difficult when you have religious Christian churches who do not distinguish between the genuinely born again and those who are not. The church must constantly be available as a court, to hear and judge moral issues and wrongs between brethren. They must act on Christ's directive, and be strong enough to discern guilt and defend the righteous. Then, upon setting out a righteous remedial course, if this is not received and acted on, declare the guilty as "a heathen and a Publican" (unbeliever).

This places the pronounced *"heathen and a Publican,"* to be dealt with as an unbeliever in an unequally yoked marriage. The same divorce rulings apply should a divorce take place, as covered in verse fifteen.

Should anyone not see this, they are disregarding Christ's words as stated in Matthew 18:17: "Let him be unto thee as an heathen man and a publican." "Let him be unto thee," is more than simply naming a so judged person. It is a directive as to how we should classify and treat this person. Due to their actions and inactions per church-governed judgment, they are to be treated as an unbeliever.

Point Two: Believers with Wrong Understandings

The first point all clergy and leadership should come to grips with is their responsibility to preach the whole council of God (Acts 20:27). If you conclude the above writings to be scriptural and correct, even if your church affiliation has differing views, become a servant of God and not of men! Teach your people biblical bondage-breaking truth. This is our godly responsibility!

Our God spoke of Levi, the chosen head of the priesthood, "For the priest's lips should keep knowledge, and they should seek the law at his mouth: for he is the messenger of the Lord of hosts" (Malachi 2:7). I am knowledgeable that most or 90 percent of churches have a limited theology regarding this vital topic, which affects so many. Be responsible, teach the truth.

We pray for the "anointing" upon our ministry. The intent of the anointing of the Holy Spirit is found in Isaiah 61:1: "The Spirit of the Lord God is upon me; because the Lord hath anointed me to preach good tidings unto the meek; he hath sent me to bind up the brokenhearted, to proclaim liberty to the captives, and the opening of the prison to them that are bound." Preach the total truth and set captives free. Make your congregation knowledgeable as to this vital topic!

Point Three: Limited and Unscriptural Ministry Structure

The ministry structure of most churches is extremely limited when compared to scriptural realities. My book, *Five-fold Ministry Churches,* deals with this topic in depth. This horrible lack is profoundly sad and has horrible negative consequences. One result of this impoverished ministry structure is an inability to deal with the believer's problems in depth. To be concise, this type of care takes real time.

All churches without a multiple ministering eldership are out of order (unless growing and heading towards this). Paul tells Titus, "For this cause left I thee in Crete, that you should set in order the things that are wanting, and ordain elders in every city, as I had appointed thee" (Titus 1:5). Clearly, all churches need a multiple eldership to be "in order."

This eldership needs to be involved in the ministry to the flock and not be an advisory group to a "pastor," as a board of non-ministering so-called elders. In Acts 20:17, Paul asked the *elders* (plural and normal) of Ephesus to meet with him, and the rest of the chapter is directed to these elders. In verse 28, Paul tells these plural elders that they are all to "Take heed therefore unto yourselves, and to all the flock, over which the Holy Ghost hath made you overseers, to feed the church of God."

All of them were to feed the church. All of these plural elders were to take the oversight. All of them were to be available with Godly maturity and wisdom to deal with those who "take it to the church." This eldership was made up of called ministries, as well as those who "desired to be an elder" (1 Timothy 3:1), meeting certain standards of qualification (1 Timothy 3:2–6, 1 Peter 5:1, Titus 1:5–9).

Elders are to have a certain maturity standard and not be novices. You cannot purchase them at a local supermarket, but need to raise them up. All elders should be matured past the "Babe" stage in knowledge (Hebrews 5:12–6:2), and should all be capable of teaching: "Therefore leaving the principles of the doctrine of Christ, let us go on unto perfection; not laying again the foundation of repentance from dead works, and of faith toward God, Of the doctrine of baptisms, and of laying on of hands, and of resurrection of the dead, and of eternal judgment." They are "babes," until knowledgeable (Hebrews 5:12).

All churches should be striving to conform to this multiple norm set out in Holy Writ, however, this will not be until ministries will bow to God's Word, instead of observing the status quo of the usual existence. Neither can this multiple ministering eldership be applied, until we humbly come to Philippians 2:3: "Let nothing be done through strife or vainglory; but in lowliness of mind let each esteem other better than themselves."

As long as some take the pastor role and esteem themselves to be the only ones capable of ministering to the real practical needs of people and applying God's Word to the considerations involved, the genuine answers are a long way off.

Only with a multiple ministering eldership, which is God's scriptural norm, will we be capable of dealing with the congregational problems. Only then can we put up the sign: "Problem solvers available, church court is open." Until then, we will be just like Moses, until Jethro came along with holy wisdom and said in Exodus 18:13–14, "And it came to pass on the morrow, that Moses sat to judge the people: and the people stood by Moses from the morning unto the evening. And when Moses' father in law saw all that he did to the people, he said, What is this thing that thou doest to the people? why do you sit alone, and all the people stand by thee from morning unto even"? Moses changed and we should also, out of the love of God and genuine love for His people, our fellow believers.

Point Four: Believers Invited to Attend Church Court

Some might say, "We have that possibility available," while few in reality do. To prove this, when is the last time you heard an invitation and teaching to bring family of God problems to the church as a refuge for problem solving? How many churches have the plural ministering elders available for such a task? How many churches will take an authoritarian position and demand that the party complained about must attend and this demand is not negotiable?

How many churches have the multitude of council available to achieve God's balanced wisdom? Proverbs 11:14 says, "Where no counsel is, the people fall: but in the multitude of counselors there is safety." Is there safety for your flock? As a minister, will you take the responsibility to follow God's Word and set this in order?

I still remember as a young working minister doing work for a fellow professed believer. He would not pay me what was agreed to. He robbed me of a just and needed income. After seeking God and prayerfully searching the Word, I determined to take him to the church. If he would not attend a church hearing, I planned to take him to the world court.

I went to the leadership of his church affiliation and requested this hearing upon explaining the substantial loss to my needed family income. First, it was made clear that they preferred to not get involved, but did so after my quoting Matthew Chapter 18. Then they struggled as to who should attend the hearing, this not being the norm (in a full gospel denomination). Then when the meeting took place, they all agreed to my claim, but cut the amount in half, not wanting to be too hard on the other "weak" brother at my expense. The real weak brothers ran the leadership meeting. They damaged the offending brother as well. Unfortunately, this is often the norm.

Point Five: Churches Not Pronouncing Guilt and Innocence from the Pulpit in Divorce

How many people went through a divorce in the average city church during the last twenty years? How often have you heard a guilt or innocence proclamation? Point made! No righteous judgment and leadership accountability in this matter. How many divorced believers walk around with the pain of being under a shadow of critique because the leadership never genuinely got involved and the church court was closed?

Often the eyes are shut and the ears of the leadership are closed while people get a divorce. Often they do not know the facts, avoiding involvement. Often they hear partially and conclude without hearing from both parties. Proverbs 18:13 says, "He that answers a matter before he hears it, it is folly and shame unto him."

Please do not talk about the poor, overworked preacher. Wrong, unscriptural church government structures and denial of God's Word, as written in Titus 1:5, produces this very problem!

I know of a very sensitive and astute backslidden professional person in my life, who just "slipped away" with no follow-up from the church they attended, following a divorcement. No holy dealings were discussed or judgment given. He is now un-churched. How many marriages are in danger right now and heading for an eventual divorce? Have you, pastor and eldership, advised your people that the church remedial court is open?

Point Six: Church Leadership Deferring from Judging Sin and Wrong

We need to see that godly judgment is carried out by a multiple eldership in our churches! This is God's grace and mercy for an ultimate good end. We need to perform and establish righteous judgment among the people of God.

We need to judge others and ourselves with the principles of preservation, love, and restoration in mind.

First, we must judge ourselves, and when we do not, God will. "For this cause many are weak and sickly among you, and many sleep" (1 Corinthians 11:30). This same principle applies to the church and the leadership thereof, when they refuse to judge and correct issues of wrong. People die due to our non-judgment (Jeremiah 5:5). Please, face responsibility and do not wimp out.

"For I verily, as absent in body, but present in spirit, have judged already, as though I were present, concerning him that hath so done this deed, In the name of our Lord Jesus Christ, when ye are gathered together, and my spirit, with the power of our Lord Jesus Christ To deliver such an one unto Satan for the destruction of the flesh, that the spirit *may be* saved in the day of the Lord Jesus" (1 Corinthians 5:3–5). The judgment enacted was for the good of those involved, hopefully bringing change.

Our God clearly sets out His heart and states He will make covenant with those who exercise true judgment. We find in Isaiah 61:8, "*For I the Lord love judgment,* I hate robbery for burnt offering; and I will direct their work in truth, and I will make an everlasting covenant with them."

Lastly, whatever happened to the obedient application of 1 Corinthians 5:11 12? But now I have written unto you not to keep company, if any man that is called a brother be a fornicator, or covetous, or an idolater, or a railer (abusive mocker), or a drunkard, or an extortioner; with such an one not to eat. For what have I to do to judge them also that are without? do not ye judge them that are within?

Do ye not? This is not possible without a scriptural ministry structure.

May we love our people enough to learn the principles and theology of godly judgment in the church. Then apply these in the arena of marital problems and divorce. It is nearly impossible to make this a reality without a multiple ministering leadership.

Point Seven: Church Leadership Deferring from Public Declaration

Deferring from publically declaring the results of church dealings with erring people may seem as loving and gracious to some, but in fact is sin before a Holy God. Our LORD said the person denying holy directives in the face of problems is to be "treated as an unbeliever, and a heathen."

Paul also taught in God's Holy Word in Romans 16:17, "Now I beseech you, brethren, mark them which cause divisions and offences contrary to the doctrine which ye have learned; and avoid them." This avoidance was for two reasons. The first was to protect the flock from wrong-minded people. The second reason for avoidance was out of a genuine love for the errant. Punishment with prayer may get them back on track.

Unfortunately, many regard this as too extreme. By their scripturally attested disobedience, they state our ways are higher than God's ways, versus the truth. Our God righteously states in Isaiah 55:9, "For as the heavens are higher than the earth, so are my ways higher than your ways, and my thoughts than your thoughts." Obedience in

these difficult waters of life is better than religious sacrifice
(1 Samuel 15:12).

Humbly Attending

It is a sin to be silent, denying the involvement of others when necessary. This unwillingness expresses a loveless and ungodly wrong heartedness. None should deny the request of a hurting spouse to attend counseling. We do not have the right to withhold ourselves from honest, open, and caring conversation. Anyone who is unwilling to do so is ungodly and are in the same category as the heathens and publicans who will not listen to the church and must be treated as such.

Substitute Solution

If you cannot find a mature multiple eldership church, with the strength or heart needed to face and address difficult marriage discussions, consider a second choice alternative. Find the most mature and godly saint who is comparable to a functional elder to talk to. I know there are hurting people out there right now, who are struggling in pain and looking for answers.

Some are greatly damaged because their church leadership has advised them to attend secular counseling or psychologists. Unless these professional people are mature in the LORD, this sending is to unspiritual and ungodly help, while abdicating their God-given chair of responsibility. Secondly, it takes a lot of finances for these professional services. Many people with marriage problems also face financial challenges.

May the LORD help us to face our responsibility. Heal the hurting by listening and helping them walk through problems to victory. Churches can also be ministering to un-churched as well. This can be a loving holy outreach, using mature believers and elders. There are volumes of people out there in marital and relational pain.

Know this: God loves all of humanity and sent His Son Jesus Christ to die on a cross because He loves the world. He does not want any to perish, but wants all to have eternal life (2 Peter 3:9).

We need to set a godly example to the world by caring for the broken and wounded, which is glorifying to our God. Godly examples of righteous dealings with families and divorce matters will result with many more people, having their names written in the Book of Life. These written therein gain eternal life with Christ and avoid an awful hell (Revelation 20:12).

REAL LOVE, FACING RESPONSIBILITY

Church, Preacher's, and Eldership Responsibility

Very few churches teach the contents of 1 Corinthians Chapter 7. Why not? Many do not teach the contents of Matthew 18, or 1 Corinthians Chapter 5 about church judgment. Why not? They will not judge a wayward soul as a heathen and a publican. Why not? Does that seem to be too direct?

We must teach and apply all scriptural truths. We may not be selective by ignoring scriptural portions by reasoning them away. Bad doctrine is due to using a single or a few texts which apply to a subject.

For those who find this presentation to be difficult, please study the scriptures referred thoroughly in context. If the study leads one to "transgress the traditions of the elders," stand for truth. Our LORD did just that albeit He was crucified as all who stand for truth will partake of (Matthew 5:2).

If we love Jesus, we will feed His lambs and His sheep. We will also break bondages and open prison doors and let captives go free (Isaiah 61:1–2). We will love the saints and people Christ died for. We will not just "preach," but will weep with those who weep, and we will carry each other's burdens.

I conclude that this absence of not strongly focusing on those who are in marital trouble is due to scriptural ignorance. This is also due to the fear of man, which is much worse, or a loveless shepherding. Regardless, there is an absence of kneeling to the holy Word of God. A disregard of the LORD of the Church and His Words by far is the worst. May we love our God and His people enough to apply scriptural realities, and bow before His throne! He is LORD!

Our LORD and Savior faced the cross and death so that the believer might have life. Should we not do all that is possible as to ministering love to His children? Our LORD Jesus said that He came to give us life, and that more abundantly John 10:10. This abundant life is tied to receiving Him, His Lordship and Kingdom. The Kingdom results only attend those who walk in Kingdom Lordship principles, with the freedom to do so.

Real Love and Ministry

How deep is the sorrow of tears in the night, of broken husbands, wives and children, passing through divorcement waters? Do we care? If we care, put on the gospel armor, declare the Holy Bible truths concerning this topic, and set men free! Stand and be counted! Be godly and raise a standard. Or perhaps we have forgotten to love our people enough to live with them and only want to preach to them and look the part of a knowledgeable "minister."

Many just strive to be known and visible as the "Right Reverend, Bishop, Doctor next to God" clergy person. Having our focus on having a standing of honor and title worthy of our calling is acceptable. We should honor those who are called of God. However, when these honor titles are carried by those who do not "weep with those who weep," they are Pharisee titles.

Our LORD taught us about some folks who were just like that: "Woe unto you, scribes and Pharisees, hypocrites! for ye pay tithe of mint and anise and cumin, and have omitted the weightier matters of the law, judgment, mercy, and faith: these ought ye to have done, and not to leave the other undone" (Matthew 23:23).

Do you consider this description and communication to be too disrespectful or hard a comparison, and does this offend you? Should the real offense not be aimed at those who carry titles and do not care for the flock by seeking out the struggling and wounded? "For the Son of man is come to save that which was lost. How think ye? if a man have an hundred sheep, and one of them be gone astray, doth he not leave the ninety and nine, and goes into the mountains, and seeks that which is gone astray? (Matthew 18:11)?

Divorce is the number one extremely painful matter among the church believers. Marriage conflict and pain including divorce is rarely dealt with as the Bible intends it to be. This topic deals with a huge area of struggle and pain within the believing community, as well as the world. The church needs to deal with this real and existing problem by setting things straight and teaching the whole counsel of God to their people, then taking genuine responsibility for the flock they claim authority over. We do so by teaching, counseling, and judging between brethren in righteousness.

Divorce badly cripples those involved in the broken marriage couple. It rips with pain. Divorce sows immense devastation in the aftermath within damaged children. This "long-term" pain is emotional and the damage done results in a spiritual disarray resulting from this dilemma as well. We must repent of accepting a church government structure that is less than what we were meant to have, so we can deal with this difficult and painful issue.

Until we have a multiple eldership church government fully released to minister, with elders who are doctrinally mature and know "the whole counsel of God" to deal with life's issues, we will not be capable of dealing with this painful dilemma. The church must deal with this life reality, rubber meet the road arena of agony and death.

Rubber Meets Road Leadership

Church believers need to be made aware of their responsibility, as well as to being accountable to those in authority over them. Believers also need to see and know that the church government is intensely interested in their personal welfare, to the degree that leadership will get involved in setting wrongs right. They need to know there is a "holy church family court," and that their leadership cares enough to get involved with their pain, struggles, and personal lives. Believers need to be aware of the church spiritual authority, which is Christ-given.

Authority Comes with Responsibility

Church leaders need to understand their God-given responsibility, which always attends holy authority. Again my friend Ernesto says, "We have no real authority unless we are under authority." Many do not relate to this. This tragedy exists due to pastors, the current predominant ministers, not having a godly scriptural knowledge of what their responsibilities are.

Current understandings limit the growth and maturing of much needed "ministering" elders. This system usually has a single central leader, with a voted-in "yes group," called a church council or board, or elders. Unfortunately, most of these elders involved have little comparison to what a biblically described elder should look and function like. Until we have this wrong and carnally non-spiritual system renovated, we are not ready to deal with this problem in the church body. Inequity, spiritual death, and wrongful struggles result within a wounded people. Often these struggles destroy the lives of genuine believers.

Without a functional scriptural church ministry structure, we have boxed ourselves into an impossible situation where we are incapable of dealing with "church body issues" in a God-intended manner. May we love our God and His people enough to seek a remedial course of action.

All of the elders must be mature and freed to take "heed unto the flock over whom the Holy Ghost has made you overseers" (Acts 20:17, 28).

God Himself Divorces People

Many will be shocked by this statement and theological presentation. This truth is not preached from the average pulpit, due to a disregard for the scriptures which state these facts. This is due to a lack in the study of this Bible topic.

God hates divorce and covenant breaking, but allows this when it is warranted. God divorces people, as stated in Malachi 2:10–13. Here, the prophet states God's Words and heart in dealing with His covenant people who have forsaken Him:

> "Have we not all one father? Hath not one God created us? Why do we deal treacherously every man against his brother, by profaning the covenant of our fathers? Judah hath dealt treacherously, and an abomination is committed in Israel and in Jerusalem; for Judah hath profaned the holiness of the LORD which he loved, and hath married the daughter of a strange god. The LORD will cut off the man that doeth this, the master and the scholar, out of the tabernacles of Jacob, and him that offers an offering unto the LORD of hosts. And this have ye done again, covering the altar of the LORD with tears."

Note that the love Judah once had has been disregarded. Note that regardless of the scholarly standing, God will remove the one who forsakes this love, including pastors and leaders.

Judah, out of which Christ was born, treacherously left off loving the LORD, and *married* the daughter of a strange god. God's promise to those covenant people was to cut them off with a radical *divorcement*. This was irrespective of scholar, minister, or leadership standing. Their religious tears and offerings did not deter God's heart or judgment. Our unchanging God did this with the heart knowledge portrayed in 1 Corinthians 5:6: "a little leaven leavens the whole lump." We need to judge right and wrong in the church when dealing with leaven. Leaven in scriptures is a type of sin. A little leaven travels through an entire bread dough, just as sin destroys the entire person.

Some will only quote the truths expressed in Malachi 2:15, where we are reminded not to deal treacherously with the wife of our youth. Also observe the contents of verse 16 where God speaks of his dislike of "putting away." These are holy directives for us to be gracious, righteous, and fair in dealing with our spouses. These scriptures apply to both husbands and abusive wives.

A wife can equally become bitter against her husband, as a husband can toward a wife. Both can ignore godly manners in dealing with marriage wrongs. A great wrong is to choose not to discuss and talk out problems, one with another. Either partner has the right to get help if needed. Both can forget genuine love as defined by 1 Corinthians 13:4–13. When bitterness enters in, by which many people are defiled, subtle things and reactions will come out to thwart and resist a holy marriage relationship (Hebrews

12:15). Should either party not be willing to address things upon request, the marriage will be in jeopardy.

Genuine, knowledgeable, godly counseling would help immensely. When one of the marriage partners inwardly "digs in their heels" and refuses to make themselves available for Godly church counseling, the marriage is on slippery ground and near divorce. The real issues are to be sorted out by those involved. When they are unable to do so, they must be dealt with by and through the church. Anyone who is unwilling to do so is ungodly.

The reality of *failure within the church regarding this subject can readily be seen. This is evident by the absence of godly church judgment.* This is verified by the absence of people being treated as a heathens or as a publican. Both the innocent and the guilty suffer because of this. The guilty suffer due to the lack of church judgment as well. This judgment would act as a guardrail on a twisting road in dangerous terrain. Setting standards along with righteous judgment may prevent some from tumbling into ravines of lifelong and eternal damage.

Eldership and Church Judgment

Let us note God's Word in Jeremiah 5:4–5: "Therefore I said, surely these are poor; they are foolish: for they know not the way of the LORD, nor the judgment of their God. I will get me unto the great men, and will speak unto them; for they have known the way of the LORD, and the 'judgment of their God': but these have altogether broken the yoke, and burst the bonds. Wherefore a lion out of the forest shall slay them."

Perhaps we lack great men who know the way of the LORD. When we lack "great men" with a good understanding of "the judgment of our God," no righteous judgment will go forth. The people will perish by lions. Here we see the reality of what Apostle Peter warned about, "Be sober, be vigilant; because your adversary the devil, as a roaring lion, walks about, seeking whom he may devour" (1Peter 5:8). Emotionally damaged Christians are an easy target for the enemy. The enemy is always present and as a roaring lion is seeking to devour.

This especially applies to those who are weak in their knowledge of the word of God.

Divorce takes place in the church as well as the world, and we need godly guidelines to deal with this tragic area of life. Our people need to be clear in their understanding that they are in the wrong if they do not involve "those in the LORD over them" (Hebrews 13:7, 17).

"Those over them" sin when they do not take their responsibility seriously and do not hold their people accountable, by avoidance of living out and facing their responsibility. They must identify and speak out against sin and wrong. Somewhere there is wrong involved within the relationship, when two believers divorce. Equally, there is wrong present when those in authority do not address this and get involved.

Israel and Marriage Dealings

To really start this topic off and get into this in greater depth, let's look at some Old Testament righteous laws given to establish a balance of loving fairness as we determine to be holy, righteous, and gracious in dealing with the saints.

Factual God-directed dealings in marital matters were done in the presence of the elders:

> "And if the man like not to take his brother's wife, then let his brother's wife go up to the gate unto the elders, and say, My husband's brother refuses to raise up unto his brother a name in Israel, he will not perform the duty of my husband's brother. Then the elders of his city shall call him, and speak unto him: and if he stand to it, and say, I like not to take her; Then shall his brother's wife come unto him in the presence of the elders, and loose his shoe from off his foot, and spit in his face, and shall answer and say, So shall it be done unto that man that will not build up his brother's house."

> Deuteronomy 25:7–9

Wrong actions were addressed, and that was before the elders. This holy directive was acted out:

> "Therefore the kinsman said unto Boaz, Buy it for thee. So he drew off his shoe. And Boaz said unto the elders, and unto all the people, Ye are witnesses this day, that I have bought all that was Elimelech's,

and all that was Chilion's and Mahlon's, of the hand of Naomi. Moreover Ruth the Moabites, the wife of Mahlon, have I purchased to be my wife, to raise up the name of the dead upon his inheritance, that the name of the dead be not cut off from among his brethren, and from the gate of his place: ye are witnesses this day. And all the people that were in the gate, and the elders, said, we are witnesses.

Ruth 4:8–11

This holy and God-orchestrated dealing was not the best kept secret in town, but a publically viewed dealing with no room for surmise or gossip. The elders and all who were present witnessed to this dealing before God and man. All the people knew of the righteous status in the Boaz and Ruth marriage.

Here we read God-given directives as to how we should deal with matters, including the rights and wrongs involving marriage and divorce. This was finalized before the elders. In this case it was settled by taking off shoes and by spitting in the face of guilty persons. Matters of right and wrong were judged and witnessed by and before elders then and should be before the elders now.

We need to see some shoes being removed in the sight of the elders. Some will immediately say, "That's Old Testament." This was God's holy directive as to how we should deal with this matter. People still have the same problems. The difference is that the past priesthood and elders are replaced with the Jesus ministry (today's five-fold ministry elders). We are told to "take it to the church" by our LORD in the New Testament. By the way, "the taking off of the shoe" signifies this is done before God on holy ground. (Exodus 3:5)

Applicable to the New Testament Church?

This is written for us today in the New Testament to the church as Christ declared in Matthew. Our LORD gave commandment about dealing with people's sins and problems involving each other.

"Moreover if thy brother shall trespass against thee, go and tell him his fault between thee and him alone: if he shall hear thee, thou hast gained thy brother. But if he will not hear thee, then take with thee one or two more, that in the mouth of two or three witnesses every word may be established. And if he shall neglect to hear them, tell it unto the church: whatsoever ye shall bind on earth shall be bound in heaven" (Matthew 18:15–18).

Our God has not changed. Consider that the laws given were to the "church" in the wilderness. Likewise, this directive was given by our LORD and Savior for the New Testament believer (Acts 7:38).

Divorce Leadership, Responsibility, and Authority

In some cases, the church has provided marriage counseling. There are well meaning and big-hearted Christian marriage counselors out there, and my prayer is that they should become knowledgeable of the truths presented herein. However, this counseling must include the church eldership upholding godliness with consequences to all.

Both the church leadership and the believer must acknowledge the church authority realm which comes with responsibility. Listening with care and with prayerful counseling is charitable. This is godly and brotherly love in action to help sort out problems. This also shows humility and a submissive spirit on the part of those seeking counseling. However, we the eldership have the great responsibility of dealing with these matters.

The church eldership is to judge matters of wrongdoing and see that these areas are corrected. This also includes wrongdoing by the believer toward the unbeliever. Then, if the unrepentant person will not listen and continues in their course of sin and error, the ministry elders must declare their guilt, setting matters aright for all to see.

Apostle Paul chided the Corinthian church: "Do not ye judge them that are within?" (1 Corinthians 5:12). When genuine wrong is determined and the guilty party is unyielding to righteousness and unrepentant, we must declare them as unrighteous, and stand with the righteous believer. There are several truths in Matthew, Chapter 18 we must consider when dealing with the wrongs and heartaches perpetrated against the saints.

First: We need to understand this directive is just as valid if it read, "If your sister trespasses against thee," and applies regardless of gender. The laws of righteousness apply to men and women alike. Salvation is an individual matter. A woman may be saved while her husband is not (1 Corinthians 7:13). A wife may also be guilty of pushing a husband out of the door.

I have seen a female ministry use the gospel and faith issues as an excuse to dump a peaceable unsaved husband when she wanted another man whom she had met in her prison ministry. I have also known of a prophetess who divorced her unsaved husband saying, "I can serve God better alone." Both of their ministries died shortly after.

Second: Both the wife and husband need to find a shelter of righteous protection and a defense against right and wrong in the "church." Both genders may "take it to the church" when destructive conditions exist. Eldership must be impartial in righteously dealing with both parties, with no "soul tie" friendship biases. We need God's wisdom and righteousness in these events.

Third: This church defense and righteous protection in the face of marriage wrongs is upheld in the Old Testament as well as the New. "Let his brother's wife go up to the gate unto the elders, and say," (Deuteronomy 25:7) She approached the elders to receive righteous judgment, and that in a matter regarding marriage. The church is to be approachable and a refuge for those who are being wronged and abused in a "Christian" marriage.

If we are not open to and encouraging this, we are co-responsible for the demise of the marriage and the eventual divorce, because we did not defend the innocent and set a standard of righteousness. Out of our love for God and man, we must see our responsibilities in this area. This is part of taking heed over the flock. Our LORD Jesus said hirelings run from difficult circumstances. True shepherds defend the flock (John 10:12).

Fourth: In this holy process, after an in-depth dealing, should you conclude that one of the partners of the marriage is an innocent victim, willing to address any potential area of wrong doing. Meanwhile their spouse is bound up with a wrong focus of bitterness or other ungodly actions. Should the unwilling spouse be counseled to address issues in the marriage, and then demonstrate their choice of not responding in humility by: avoiding personal genuine conversation, or refusing to address issues that are important to their spouse, acting out of a wrong spirit, or by avoiding meetings with others or the church? Their refusal and unwillingness to respond in a loving and positive manner must be confronted. We must know the genuine rights of and uphold the injured. Those acting outside of the laws of godly love with destructive anger or inaction must be confronted. Defending the wounded is a godly requirement for all leadership.

An unwillingness to accept holy, God-provided church ministry counseling is a sin. Ignoring requests to remedy pain and problem areas denies the believer their just, God-given rights. In such a case, the church must act out their responsibility. One of the wrongdoings listed among a list of sinful doings is the sin of being "implacable." The verse states: "Without understanding, covenant breakers, without natural affection, implacable, unmerciful" (Romans 1:31). The word "implacable" describes a person who has no heart to hear or be cooperative in efforts to achieve healing leading to unity. This is usually seen with those who deny genuine heartfelt communication, not striving for a genuine, loving, marriage relationship.

Love wants to understand and hear out difficulties to bring peace and unity. Should this not be the case, we the leadership must be aware of our responsibility which comes with the authority we took over others. If you are under a leadership who does not submit to Bible-directed responsibilities, find a different church.

Problems attend most marriages and both parties will have faults. The main problem arises when one person or both will not address the problems with love and integrity. May the LORD grant us wisdom in these matters.

Fifth: In this case, when one of them refuses to acknowledge and listen to the godly counsel of the Church, we may wind up in a position of having to treat one of them as a heathen or a publican. This means they are the same as and to be treated as an unsaved person. We have failed to apply these truths and may the LORD forgive us.

Considering this, our judgment had better be righteous. The people submitting to the church for judgment had better be transparent and godly. If the church binds a righteous judgment on earth, it will be bound in heaven. Our God will not honor an unrighteous judgment from the earth. We need to have godly, mature, responsible under God ministries and elders. Taking heed of the flock is serious business. The flock may take God and holiness more seriously, when the ministry and leadership does.

The one who ignores the church's authority is to be treated as, and shall be as a believer dwelling with an unbeliever. The Matthew 18:17 heathen and a publican unbeliever, will now also considered as belonging to the "unbeliever" category of I Corinthians 7:12–15. Now we are dealing with the same rules of the "unequally yoked" written in these verses. Treating the person who will not listen to the church as an unbeliever is according to the commandment of Christ to you and I.

Sixth: Taking someone to the church was a directive and command and not merely an option. In my observation it is a rare occasion when someone acts on this holy directive. Most treat this Christ-given directive as an option to ignore at will. We sin by not following this directive.

The church we are linked to or turn to would hopefully be a Bible knowledgeable church, upholding godly standards.

Seventh: I have also seen this wrong being acted out against an unbeliever when a wrongful believer wants out of the relationship for wrong reasons. A righteous church judgment in such a case might defrock the "believer" from hypocrisy and ultimately bring salvation to an unbeliever witnessing righteous dealings.

DIVORCING CHRISTIAN HEATHENS

Unrighteous Conduct, Ignoring Church Holy Directives

Hear the Words from our Lord Jesus Himself. These Words apply to a person who will not yield to godly counsel from the church leadership. "but if he neglect to hear the church, let him be unto thee as an heathen man and a publican." (Matthew 18:17). Should one be judged as such, at Christ's command, they should be treated as an unbeliever. They are now to be an "esteemed unbeliever," living with a Christian brother or sister, in the matter of separation and divorce. They belong to the category of people who are "not under bondage" should a divorce take place, and are freed to remarry.

Should an eventual divorce result with the genuine godly Christian having done their godly all to achieve a happy home with a godly life on their part, they are free to divorce and remarry.

We must determine the "saved" status of the people we are dealing with when counseling marriage problems. The apostle Paul made this distinction mandatory in 1 Corinthians chapter seven.

Also, there is a difference between judging and being judgmental. Judging corrects wrong and leads to life, while having a judgmental attitude leads to death. We need to apply this distinction correctly in the church.

We must have the church take their God-directed responsibility of addressing wrongs, with the intent of protecting the righteous. Help them obtain a righteous and godly peace. The believer must with holy responsibility "take it to the church." The church must declare a public judgment when a supposed believer does not demonstrate a genuine godly response to wrongs addressed. When the church does not judge, they are failing the believers and God himself.

The church and ministry who do not attend to and do not welcome being involved in dealing with people's problems, are walking in "sin." They are disregarding their responsibilities under God. They should not take a visible authority position without taking a functional responsibility for those over whom they have allowed themselves to be placed in authority over. By the non-action of ungodly leadership, the damaged Christian is crucified a second time after being injured by the abusive or wrongful marriage relationship they parted from.

Our LORD has told the church what their responsibility is, to hear and judge matters. They need to conclude the matter and outcome. In the case of an unhearing person, this includes declaring a judgment with a strong result. Declaring a person as a heathen and publican is a strong indictment. The commandment to declare the non-submissive ungodly Christian as a heathen and publican is followed with, "Verily I say unto you, Whatsoever ye shall bind on earth shall be bound in heaven: and whatsoever ye shall loose on earth shall be loosed in heaven." Church! Ministry! Take your responsibilities seriously. God does when we do.

Genuine Ministry Oversight

Our LORD Jesus Christ ascended to heaven and gave five differing ministries to the church. (Ephesians 5:8, 11) The Holy Spirit will provide God appointed eldership to feed and oversee the flock, when believers yield to Him. (Acts 20:17, 28)

We are told in Hebrews 13:17 to: *"Obey them that have the rule over you, and submit yourselves: for they watch for your souls, as they that must give account, that they may do it with joy, and not with grief: for that is unprofitable for you."* When a difficult marriage partner refuses to attend counseling discussions with those "in the LORD over you," they are disregarding Holy Ghost (God) made eldership and the church's Christ-given ministry government (should they be saved and mature elders). In Ezekiel 44:8, God berated the people for setting a leadership over themselves who were ungodly. Have you?

We need to be sure we are in submission to genuine "Holy Ghost-made" eldership. True ministry leadership will know and counsel according to God's Holy Word principles. Mature eldership ministry will align with biblical elder descriptions (1 Timothy 3:1–10, Titus 1:5–9, Hebrews 5:12–6:2).

We must see the vast difference between the two differently identified groups addressed in 1 Corinthians chapter 7. We must see which appropriate and applicable laws apply, should a divorce take place. The difference defines the status of both marriage partners regarding the possibility of remarriage.

Do not confuse merely being religious with being saved. There are numerous Christian churches with varying quantities of unsaved people. I personally left a "Calvinistic" church behind where the preacher, Board of elders, and followers mocked the term "born again," and few were. I was formally excommunicated by these people. My crime was that I had subjected myself to being baptized as a believer after reading, "Baptism is the answer of a clean conscience before God" (1 Peter 3:21). I knew my conscience was not clean before personally accepting Christ. I knew that my well meaning parents could not answer for my conscience. Have you considered answering our Lord?

The pastor when questioned said, "You cannot know whether you will obtain heaven until you are dead and judged." It was sad that he did not know a sure salvation, but praise God! I know he is wrong because I know God's promise and His Word. I am saved! We are told in the gospel of John, "Verily, verily, I say unto you, He that hears my word, and believeth on him that sent me, hath everlasting life, and shall not come into condemnation; but is passed from death unto life" (John 5:24). God's spirit witnesses with my spirit (Romans 8:15–16).

Conclusion to Second Grounds for Divorce

The conclusion of this matter is: when a believer has done their godly all, in dealing with a so-called believer or when a self proclaimed Christian *who will not attend or listen to* and respect holy loving and graciously truthful church counseling and directives, they are now to be treated as an unbeliever.

When a person who is declared by the church to be an unbeliever, because they disregarded and did not embrace godly counsel and principles. Should their conduct not contribute to affecting a peaceful home for the believer to reside in. Should the marriage fail and a divorce take place as a result of this, the result is a God honored and provided option by His Word. He allows us a life of peace and joy. He draws us to green pastures and is a restorer of the soul.

This calling to peace demands that the believer needs to deal with their circumstances in such a manner that a peaceful environment will result.

Step to Daylight, Peace, and Hope for Tomorrow

The course to achieving peace and hope for a different tomorrow lies in following the steps directed by the LORD Jesus as outlined in Matthew chapter 18. Do what Our LORD Jesus said: "Take it to the church." However, you will be limited in applying these steps in a practical manner unless one is involved with a righteous church ministry leadership.

Only a genuine godly leadership will apply God's Word. Some churches hold the theology of "Wives submit yourselves unto your husbands" without the balancing words of "Husbands love your wives," and the softening words of "Submitting yourselves one to another in the fear of God," which balances a domineering stance, and leaves some room for discussion (Ephesians 5:21–25).

Then, they totally forget to preach the most important Bible texts, which apply to all Christian relationships; and, especially in marriage, these must be applied by both parties.

"Charity suffers long, and is kind; charity envies not; charity vaunts not itself, is not puffed up, Doth not behave itself unseemly, seeks not her own, is not easily provoked, thinks no evil; Rejoices not in iniquity, but rejoices in the truth; Bears all things, believeth all things, hopes all things, endures all things. Charity never fails…"

1 Corinthians 13:4–8

When these truths are accepted and applied, we have God's recipe for a great marriage. A genuinely godly saved person will correct wrongs addressed being guided by the foregoing truths.

Should the actual reason for the divorce be that one has their heart set on a different adulterous third party, the result will be a lack of peace with a guilty shadow over their lives. If the believer applied an unrighteous "Christian" force to alienate the unbeliever, then no peace will attend the resulting divorce. We cannot force "faith," but can only witness to it.

Some of these actions observed include and are not limited to: If one constantly pushes gospel tracts under their spouse's breakfast plate, daily forces loud gospel music into their ears, while continually quoting a bunch of critical "thou shalt" scriptures, thereby destroying the peace of the unbeliever, thereby forcing them out of the door as a result of insensitive actions. The Christian believer will have no peace upon the eventual divorce. We must love them in their state of unbelief, as we also demand a loving and considerate response from them towards us, in the practicing of our faith.

If the marriage breaks up and the believer was not genuinely praying and interceding for the soul of the unbeliever, they will reap the result of a wrong heartedness, a divorce with no peace. Nevertheless, know your right to a life of peace and claim that, walking with the Lord.

A person who was divorced and saved afterward is free from their past failures, which are washed by the cross. They should address restitution and responsibility areas where possible.

I have heard of several groups which will judge that a remarried person having experienced a divorce prior to be saved is living in adultery. This erroneous doctrinal outlook ignores David's adultery with Bathsheba. This viewpoint denies the power of the blood for the new creature in Christ Jesus. This opinion should also include that a murderer like Paul should not preach, while God had him write half of the New Testament. Imposing this opinion as a law, disregards those who have a righteous divorce due to godly dealings.

Two Christian believers should work out their differences through the church eldership. If one refuses to hear and act from such godly counsel, and the marriage dissolves the freed believer may remarry.

"Art thou loosed (freed) from a wife? seek not a wife. 28a But and if thou marry, thou hast not sinned" (1 Corinthians 7:27, 28). Should a person follow the God-given prescription addressed herein for resolving problems, and the marriage ends due to a partner who does not act out a godly response bringing a peaceful resolution by not listening to church counseling, the believer is freed.

Should the marriage to one classified as an unbeliever or non-equally yoked relationship disintegrate, while the child of God has righteously done their part in a Godly fashion, and they become "loosed" from the marriage, they may remarry. Should they remarry, their genuine godliness will be evidenced when they obey the scriptural admonishment, "Only in the LORD," by marrying a genuine believer who has demonstrated a love for Jesus and is saved (1 Corinthians 7:39).

Those who disagree with these clearly set out scripturally supported views portray an unjust God. They depict a god with unrighteousness, allowing the result of a person with ungodly actions to rob a godly person of joy and a godly healthy marriage. They honor the effect of ungodliness and justify this, thereby bringing bondage to a child of God.

Loosed From

Becoming loosed from a marriage is different than becoming a widow or widower, by reason of the death of a mate. The Greek word "loosed" is G3089 *luo*, meaning "A primary verb"; to "loosen" (literally or figuratively): break (up), destroy, dissolve, loose, melt, put off. This word is also taken from G4486 *hrace'-so*, and G2608; to "break," "wreck," or "crack," that is, (especially) to *sunder* (by *separation* of the parts); and G2352 a *shattering* to minute fragments; - break, burst, rend, tear. (Strong's Concordance)

It is clear from the above that *this involved a breaking of a marriage with both parties being very much alive.* The choice of entering into another marriage after this "breaking," is up to the believer; however, one must consider the scriptural guidelines set out. Marry if you will but only to a believer "in the LORD."

The admonition from Paul to consider skipping a remarriage and staying celibate certainly is an option that saves one the problems associated with a future marriage. Paul as a bachelor observed the garden weeding and maintenance factor to most marriages. Genuine weeding takes a prayerful getting on your knees work. Nevertheless, Paul also taught: "But if they cannot contain, let them marry: for it is better to marry than to burn." (1 Corinthians 7:9) Also Paul states, "But if any man think that he behaves himself uncomely toward his virgin, if she pass the flower of her age, and need so require, let him do what he will, he sins not. Let them marry" (1 Corinthians 7:36).

Marriage addresses several needs, including a very basic human need, a sex drive. Behaving himself "uncomely towards his virgin" (a state of a sexless activity while struggling with desire) means he or she is not handling or containing their sexual inertia very well. Here Paul says if a person is of age and is not handling their state of celibacy or "virginity" very well, then they should consider finding a spouse and getting married (not the only reason for marriage).

Even our LORD Jesus addressed this issue of sexual appetite. He addressed this when he said, "But I say unto you, That whosoever shall put away his wife, saving for the cause of fornication, causes her to commit adultery" (Matthew 5:32).

How does a wrongful putting away of a wife "cause her to commit adultery"? It certainly is not due to an arm being twisted behind her back saying "go and get involved with fornication." It is because this leaves her in a vulnerable position of not having sexual and emotional needs satisfied, and then being tempted to address these needs in a sinful manner. I realize marriage also has many other factual needs attached, such as sharing, companionship, etcetera.

Divorced Ministry

Some churches do not allow genuine God-called ministry people to continue in public ministry if they experience a divorce, regardless of why. There are a number of factors to consider in this case. First of all, when their spouse is involved with adultery, the affected ministry needs to be upheld and esteemed. Secondly, these churches completely deny and avoid God's Word, that some have forsaken a wife for the gospel's sake (Matthew 19:29). A righteous husband, minister and all will heed the admonishment of Paul, "but if any provide not for his own, and specially for those of his own house, he hath denied the faith, and is worse than an infidel" (1 Timothy 5:8). Obviously, this forsaking was not an ungodly directive contrary to God's Word, to not care for the wife. The Christ stated forsaking had eternal rewards. This forsaking was due to standing for godly values.

Then we have the morally failed ministry.

A sinful minister having a demonstrated proven sin should not be ministering until this has been rectified. All sinners can be restored, including believers. David was after adultery and murder.

The question is, does God forgive sin when the sinner repents? Repenting would include one doing their godly all to restore and mitigate damage done due to the sin. Yes, according to 1 John 1:9, God forgives our sins when we have genuinely repented. A repentant divorced person should lovingly do all they are capable of, including attempting a restoration of the past marriage. True repentance will always be accompanied by humility. Having been convicted of wrongdoing and genuinely repenting would cause one to attempt obtaining some church counseling to deal with the relationship. At least repent and ask forgiveness for wrongdoing, thereby ministering grace to the offended past spouse. If circumstances allow, be responsible as to others and especially the children as well. Consider how they are affected by the past divorce.

Should a genuinely repenting person have made every effort to reconcile, God's grace reaches out to them. Can they remarry? Should a genuine repentance be there and all efforts for reconciliation been made towards God and man, I believe God's Word applies due to the blood and grace.

Is such a view biblical? What is the Bible proof of this opinion? Look at David, who was an adulterer and murderer, who after severely repenting, became a man after God's heart and turned the nation back to God (Psalm 51). David fulfilled his ministry after adultery and failure. He righteously and graciously embraced the widowed "Bathsheba," following a genuine God-accepted repentance.

David married other wives, while becoming *a man after his own heart, to be captain over his people,* a superb worshipping man of God and a prophet (1 Samuel 13:14).

Should a genuinely repentant God-called minister then still be denied the right to public ministry? The church should carefully determine their actions of repentance. No, the call of God and burden of ministry does not change. God's grace and truth both apply. Our LORD brought both grace and truth into this world as John the Baptist stated (John 1:17). David constructed the tabernacle of worship after failure (via Solomon), and our LORD still speaks of this in Acts chapter 15. True repentance is met with the shed blood and holy blood-bought grace. Genuine God-called ministers are not "bullet proof," and are subject to human failure. God never calls people to the ministry who are perfect. He perfects the ministry.

The real test is, how true is the repentance? We must discern this when sin is involved. People will trip and fail. This is why 1 John 1:9 was written. Failure does not automatically mean one is removed from a future God-ordained calling. Mostly all of God's ministers have been shown with their failures, including Moses, Elijah, and Paul. Our God corrected and continued to use all of them in ministry.

To judge that the one sin committed, being adultery is the sin which removes a person forever from ministry is a man-made, unscriptural conclusion. The issue here is not so much about the sin and failure that took place. The real issue is what did the person involved do after the failure. Did they repent and make every effort possible to affect restitution? That is the real question. David demonstrated that.

For the mistreated and wounded, the one comfort is that our God will know the truth of this matter. We stand or fall before Him. We cannot deceive Him. He knows the real truth of the matter. When failure overtakes you and conviction comes, yield and repent. Do not quit! This is the reason our God portrayed His greatest ministers with their failures. It is only by His mercy that any of us stand.

For the hardened critiques, may you acknowledge the truths of Galatians 6, "1 Brethren, if a man be overtaken in a fault, ye which are spiritual, restore such an one in the spirit of meekness; considering thyself, lest thou also be tempted. Bear ye one another's burdens, and so fulfill the law of Christ. For if a man think himself to be something, when he is nothing, he deceives himself. But let every man prove his own work, and then shall he have rejoicing in himself alone, and not in another." This scripture describes the humility which should attend restoration. This humility states that we are all capable of transgression. Only a wrongful, spiritual pride-saturated person denies this truth. May we weep with others and lift them up from failure, bearing each other's burdens.

I will never forget how the leader of a 600 member ministerial I belonged to for years demeaned and castigated any and all divorced ministries at a conference. The following year, he changed his tune and theology, due to his son getting divorced. May we walk softly.

Failure?

David was a God-ordained prophet as well as a king. David's understanding was that our holy God perfects the ministry. "The Lord will perfect that which concerns me: thy mercy, O Lord endures for ever: forsake not the works of thine own hands" (Psalm 138:8). Also, "As for God, his way is perfect; the word of the Lord is tried: he is a buckler to all them that trust in him. For who is God, save the Lord? and who is a rock, save our God? God is my strength and power: and he makes my way perfect" (2 Samuel 22:31–33).

Our merciful God is awesome. His grace meets the penitent. "It is of the Lord's mercies that we are not consumed, because his compassions fail not. They are new every morning: great is thy faithfulness" (Lamentations 3:22–23). He knows our frame that we are just people (Psalm 103:14). Our God graciously states, "The steps of a good man are ordered by the Lord: and he delights in his way. Though he fall, he shall not be utterly cast down: for the Lord upholds him with his hand" (Psalm 37:23–24). When God lifts up the failed preacher, may we not resist His lifting.

Saints of God, believe in God's severity in judgment as well as His grace to the genuinely penitent. He does not give up on us. We are tempted to give up on Him. The steadfast love of the Lord never fails:

> "Remembering mine affliction and my misery, the wormwood and the gall. My soul hath them still in remembrance, and is humbled in me. This I recall to

my mind, therefore have I hope. It is of the Lord's mercies that we are not consumed, because his compassions fail not. They are new every morning: great is thy faithfulness. The Lord is my portion, says my soul; therefore will I hope in him. "

Lamentations 3:19–24

May thy kingdom come on earth as it is in heaven. May all of His saints with a heartfelt joy say, "What a day that will be when my Jesus I shall see, when I look upon His face, the one who saved me by His grace."

Surely his salvation is nigh them that fear him; that glory may dwell in our land. Mercy and truth are met together; righteousness and peace have kissed each other. Truth shall spring out of the earth; and righteousness shall look down from heaven. Yea, the Lord shall give that which is good; and our land shall yield her increase. Righteousness shall go before him; and shall set us in the way of his steps.

Psalm 85:9

Apostle John Devries

AFTERWORD

Many people struggle with divorce and remarriage questions. This is especially difficult for the true believer. The believer and church need to know what is right before God and apply New Testament teachings regarding this important topic. Much is misunderstood regarding this topic.

The New Testament churches we read about seem to be so different from what we experience today. These churches blossomed and grew with a gospel explosion so that people said, "These that have turned the world upside down are come hither also" (Acts 17:6). They experienced having a great unity, with thousands being added constantly. They did this without the availability of TV, radio, planes, cars, or printing presses. What was the difference?

Much of it was the Holy Ghost power and miracles ministered by the five Christ-given ministry callings we no longer recognize, They operated in the Holy Spirit gifts which attend an experiential baptism of the Holy Spirit. Crowds believed, due to seeing the evangelist Stephen's miracle ministry.

The believers flowed at a different knowledge expectancy, being capable of teaching foundational doctrines (Hebrews 5:12). They were all invited and expected to be part of the church ministry, contributing with spiritual input and body ministry (1 Corinthians 14:26, Ephesians 4:16).

A huge difference is the church body resolved conflict, maintaining peace and unity. Leadership dealt with sin and wrong, resolving differences. (1 Co. 5:11, 1 Corinthians 6:5).

Disunity was dealt with, including marriage matters. Our Lord said this was done through a progression of discussion efforts, ultimately dealing with matters by the church when other efforts fell short of bringing resolution.

May all of the above be restored, resulting in a living church!

The author may be contacted via PO Box 0205, Post Falls, Idaho, USA, 83877–0205.